DEAR ME

Victim or Survivor
the choice is yours

M. S. Campbell

Trafford rev. 04/21/2015

 www.trafford.com

North America & international
toll-free: 1 888 232 4444 (USA & Canada)
fax: 812 355 4082

This book is dedicated to my beautiful grand-children. May they always know how much they are loved!

~~~~~~~

"And with each generation, so our souls live on and on, and our lives and all of our pain is therefore worthwhile."

Ralph Waldo Emerson

~~~~~~~

~ Acknowledgments ~

My sincere thanks to all who have supported me in writing this book. To Steve and Janice Fenner, Norma McColeman, Patricia Roy and the Malpak Arts Council.

To Jean and the late Rod MacDonald for being there for me over the years; to my brothers and sisters for all the love and support along the road and to my mother, God Bless her, she suffered so much for us.

~~~~~~~

Names in this book have been changed for reasons of my own. All quotes are so credited. All poems are my own and therefore copyrighted as part of this book.

~~~~~~~

Part of the profits from the sale of this book will be donated to East Prince Family Violence Prevention Inc., Summerside, P.E.I. .

~ TABLE OF CONTENTS ~

~ FORWARD ~

It is a terrifying but true fact, family violence has been, and continues to be, one of the worst diseases of our times. It knows no boundaries of culture, color, religion, social status or sex and yes, it is highly contagious. It kills, injures and cripples its victims, sometimes for life.

How does the cycle continue? It is simple. If you are raised with love and nurturing, gentleness and warmth, then you will raise your children with love and nurturing, gentleness and warmth. As you learn, so you are. If you are hurt, filled with fear and hate and self loathing, you will raise your children with hurt, fear, hate and self loathing.

Family violence, or abuse committed against one human by another can be called a "social disease" as it is partially due to our social structure that it continues to spread. It is learned by children from their parents and passed down from generation to generation. Even given the knowledge we have gained, family violence continues to get worse instead of better.

What follows in this book is a true story. Or, I should say it is my story. I have tried to recount a lifetime of memories, emotions and reactions to my childhood.

The truths, feelings and emotions written here are my own and the way that I reacted to my childhood is not necessarily the way that others would react. My life experience is mine alone and I am a unique human being. The way I have healed is also unique as is the story of each and every Survivor. I find that Survivors have a great deal in common. The most important being the ability to work through and get beyond the pain. We must gain the ability to trust ourselves, to feel fear and to learn that when we feel afraid and vulnerable, it doesn't necessarily mean that we will be hurt, unloved, abandoned or rejected, but that we have become part of the real world. We all experience fear from time to time and it is how we react to it that counts.

The Survivor learns that before she can love anyone, she must love herself, she must learn how to treat herself with dignity and respect. She must forgive those who have hurt her and forgive herself for being a part of that hurt. The Victim feels that her life is out of control. She feels full of hate for her abuser and she carries that hate around like a cross she must bear. In time these feelings of hate build up until she feels more and more powerless in her life. Then, she either finds a person to replace her abuser and becomes a victim, or in order to to recover that power, she herself abuses others. The violence continues on with each generation

Depression is another story. Most victims of abuse suffer from depression. The hard part is recognizing depression for the condition that it is, very common and successfully treatable. Depression has plagued me most of my life. I grew up an emotional cripple and the main obstacle in overcoming was of course myself. When I was most depressed, I didn't want help. I didn't want to admit that I was depressed, admitting it would bring shame on me.

I didn't want to feel ashamed, I just wanted to hide away in my own little world and feel sorry for myself. That is the nature of the beast, I would rather stay ill than become healthy because although I didn't want to die, I felt that I didn't deserve to enjoy and experience life. Medication could have helped me through so many horrible years, but I was either too far into the illness or too ashamed to ask for help. There is still a stigma - " she's O.K., she's just depressed" "snap out of it, get over it", or "it's all in her head".

Depression can kill. It can get so bad that the person cannot see any hope in life she ends it as she feels that living is not worth the pain. Although at times you may think that you are, you are not alone, there are millions of us. Again, if you need help, ask for it.

The secrets cannot be kept, the truth must be told. As long as the stigma remains, violence will win and abusers will hurt their victims mentally, emotionally, sexually and physically, again and again.

In this book I am baring my soul to the entire world, if you are reaching out for help, you only need to tell one trusting person, your priest, minister, doctor, teacher, someone, anyone who can help you. I only hope that within the pages of this book, you gain an understanding of what it is like to grow up in an abusive family and find solace and peace in knowing that recovery is not out of reach. If you are suffering, only you can stop the pain. If as a victim you find no peace, you will die full of hate and regret. Abusers will leave those you love behind without closure and still hating you. Victim or survivor its all up to you.

~ CHAPTER ONE ~

EIGHT LITTLE SPARROWS

So long as we are loved by others, no matter how hard our lives may be, no-one needs feel useless while she has a friend.
- Robert Louis Stevenson

They first became best friends in second grade, although they were (as Granny would say), different as day and night. Jennifer, had a head of bouncy shiny curls, framing an angelic face and long lashes that fluttered over large brown eyes. She wore clean, well fitting clothes from Eaton's or The Bay, always had lunch money and was smart as a whip. She also had loving, caring parents, Maggie wished they would adopt her. Jenny's house was cute and clean and had pretty curtains on the windows and flowers in the yard.

Maggie, on the other hand was skinny, tall for her age with ratty brown hair, a long face and sad-looking blue eyes. Her clothes were ill fitting, unclean and came in cardboard boxes or black garbage bags from the kind parishioners of the church. No-one cared which church because they "didn't go". All the kids at school would either shun her or bully her and they all called her "Raggy Maggie", but she didn't care, she had her best friend.

They were close as "two peas in a pod", inseparable. Maggie told Jenny all of her secrets and as she wasn't allowed to have kids over or to go to anyone's house, she was so happy to have Jennifer to talk to and to share with. Jennifer even knew the terrible secrets about Dad and when Maggie peed the bed, why Mom had to go away last spring and that Maggie sucked her thumb. The only one who knew about Jennifer was Granny, but Granny was acting strange these days, repeating herself and all and Maggie was thinking that Granny might tell secrets. She told Maggie that she was lucky to have Jennifer, not everyone has such a good friend.

Jenny would coach Maggie through all the spelling and math tests so they both got good marks, but the teachers always said that Maggie was a "day dreamer" and couldn't ever be as smart as Jennifer. Of course, Jenny had piano and ballet lessons and her Mom helped her with homework, she really was quite a smart girl.

Granny would say that Jennifer would likely go away to become a doctor or lawyer or some such thing. Granny would also say that the day would come when Maggie "didn't need" Jenny any more and even though it would make Maggie sad, it would mean she was growing up and standing on her own two feet.

The two girls played a game that went on from day to day for months. They pretended that they had parts in Gone With The Wind. Maggie would play Scarlet and Jenny the part of Mellie. Granny would say " They were a sight to behold, the pair of them. What with Southern accents and all the rolling of the eyes, pouting, crying and carrying on."   Maggie figured that Granny just wished she were young again so she could play along with them.

Jennifer thought it so, so stupid that Maggie had to go to bed at eight o'clock even in the summertime, the sun was still shining and all the other kids on the street would be out playing. There would be ball games at the park, skipping on the sidewalk, swimming at the pool, but the kids weren't allowed.

Over the years, the family lived in many houses. They lived on farms, in villages in big old houses and little old houses. The kids always hated moving. They would just get settled in a new place and they would have to move. Granny knew why, she told Maggie once, but of course kids being kids they didn't understand that when their father didn't pay the rent, they would have to move. In this particular house, in the summer, it would get very hot in the upstairs, and it would stink. In the hall there was a piss bucket. Emptying it was, of course, one of the jobs that no-one wanted to do so quite often it emitted the aroma of several days worth. The children were not allowed to go out to the outhouse after bedtime, so the contents of the bucket became sickening. There were two bedrooms upstairs, one for the four girls and one for the four boys. There was a curtain in between so they could talk back and forth. They didn't particularly care about changing clothes in privacy as they had no pajamas or underwear and quite often they would wear the same clothes for several days and nights. The old stained mattresses also added a distinctive odor. There were no sheets. Some of the four single beds had filthy stained pillows, others had none. The children slept two to a bed and would talk in whispers to each other, about what they would do the next day, or about when they grew up. Sometimes they would talk about tying up their father and throwing rotten tomatoes at him, they would all laugh. Sometimes they talked about running away, or about how their lives would be if he were dead. It was so sad, eight little children and wishing for the death of their own father. Eventually they would fall asleep.

More often than not, after dark, the kids would all wake in terror at the bellowing of his voice. The younger ones cried out and the older ones would try to hush them and they would talk in whispers - - "where is he, in the room?" - -" oh God, did he hit her " - - "quiet, he will hear us" - - "shush, here he comes." They could hear him unsteadily thump up the stairs.

"SHUT UP, I SAID - if you don't all shut up, I will kill you, and if I have to kill you, it will be your own damned fault - - DO YOU HEAR ME"?

"No, Ron, please don't - - leave them alone - - come back down", Mary pleaded from the hall, "Please, Ron, no - - - come down stairs"!

Maggie felt the sudden rush of adrenalin as fear gripped her. She thought he would be able to hear her heart pounding. She held her breath, plugged her ears and sand songs in her head.

"MAGGIE - - were you sucking your thumb'?- - -" Let me see it" - - "HOW DARE YOU DEFY ME"?

Maggie was so afraid that she couldn't think. She couldn't fight or run so in her own little way, she had devised a sort of survival plan, she would turn off her brain. She said nothing, just kept singing the songs in her head. She could hear nothing but the pounding of her heart and she would keep her eyes closed so that she couldn't see him.

"ANSWER ME, damn you - I'll teach you to defy me"!

He raised his hand toward her face and huge

4

sobs surfaced in her throat. The room started spinning.

The Monster took a shirt from a pile of dirty clothes in the corner and tied her right hand at the wrist to the back of the bed.

"NOW SHUT UP, damn you, I have given you kids everything. I have done without and sacrificed everything I wanted in life to raise you kids, the least you can do is SHUT UP".

All of them kept so still and so quiet, hoping he would go back downstairs. Some of them faked being asleep, imagining, hoping that he would disappear, go away, anything so the panic would stop. Some of them, being so afraid, had peed the bed which gave the hot night an even more poignant stench.

The world kept turning and no one seemed to care. Life went on, the sun rose the next morning as it did every morning, and so started another day, and another, and another.

~~~~~~~~

Sometimes the Monster decided he would be a farmer, sometimes he went to work. When he was a farmer life was harder because he was always around and always drinking, when he would find a job, life at home was much better. Mary would smile and at least was able to buy groceries, cook meals and walk down the street with some amount of dignity. The children would play and laugh like other children until his old Ford pulled into the drive, then one of them would say "here he comes" and they would all scatter like eight little sparrows being approached by a cat. The Monster never worked at a job for long. He would have another " battle of the booze" and the booze always won. Then, shortly after they would move again.

Most of the time, there was not enough food to go around and Mary quite often gave up her plate to the children. In the winter, the meal usually consisted of boiled potatoes, or spaghetti with a can of soup poured over. In the summertime, sometimes he grew a garden up the yard or neighbors would give them vegetables.

The evening meal was eaten in complete silence. No one was allowed to speak at the table. If the Monster was in a crusty mood, they weren't allowed to take their eyes from their plates.   The children and Mary ate in the kitchen, and the Monster in the room. He refused to eat with the pigs. Mary quite often ate standing up as there weren't enough chairs plus it was her job run and fetch for the Monster.   They were made to eat all of what was on their plate. Then they must ask "Please may I leave the table"? If they couldn't finish the food, they had to sit still without speaking until they could finish it which could sometimes take a long time.   The Monster would then either grant them leave, or make them sit there until he decided they could leave. If there were other children waiting outside for them, or they had homework, he would make them sit. Again they were not allowed to speak.   Sometimes he would forget that they were still at the table and have a sleep in his chair. If he fell asleep, they would have to sit at the table until he woke and then they would have to again ask to leave the table.

The girls had to do housework; boys never had to

do "women's work" and they quite often taunted and teased the girls about it. As there was no water in the house, dishes were done once a day, in the evening. The monster had usually fallen asleep in the room and Jane and Maggie, being the two oldest girls generally got the job. First, the slop bucket had to be carried out into the back yard and emptied, then water pumped and warmed up, then the dishes were washed and dried, all in compete silence. The sound of clattering dishes would send him off the deep end and all hell would break loose. Sometimes Jane and Maggie would play a game, daring each other not to laugh - laughter was not allowed. One would make faces or whisper something funny or gross and they would both bite the insides of their cheeks trying very hard not to laugh. One evening while doing dishes, Maggie coughed to try to hide the burst of laughter that had bubbled up from who knows where. "Who coughed?" the Monster yelled, "I did" said Maggie in a tiny voice, wishing she could be invisible. "Who the hell is "I did" yelled back the Monster - "get in here". She went sheepishly into the room. "HOW DARE YOU WAKE me up with your damned coughing? If you need to cough, get outside, DO YOU UNDERSTAND ME?" "Yes Dad".

They were all so afraid of the Monster that lying to keep peace just became second nature. "YOU ARE PIGS, all of you, pigs, am I right?" "ANSWER ME DAMN YOU".

"Yes Dad, you are right, we are pigs". What else could they say? If the occasion ever arose when they thought they could talk back, it was a time when the Monster was really drunk and then they would think twice knowing full well that they would have run like hell and punishment would be severe.

The children learned to lie at a very young age. Lying simply became a survival technique. They lied so he wouldn't yell, they lied so he wouldn't hurt them, or set the house on fire, or hang himself in the barn. They also lied to try for any tiny bit of acknowledgment as his child, for any small crumb of approval or praise. They lied constantly because they so desperately wanted to be loved.

In the upstairs of this house, under the slant of the roof was a closet that ran the full length on both sides. There was a wall about four feet high and the ceiling rose from there on a steep slant. The door to the "closet" was only about three feet high so that an adult would have to crouch down to enter. In that closet, the children would hide from him. If the Monster went really off the deep end, the kids would scurry into the closet and brace the door shut. Sometimes hours passed before they felt safe enough to come out and in all that time there would be only whispers between them. Even the youngest knew enough not to cry, or make any sound. The Monster in his drunken rage must have thought they had all disappeared or somehow gone away. He looked, but never found them once and they lived in that house over a year.

Christmas was not a happy time. There was no school for ten days and if the weather was bad, the kids were all trapped in the house of horrors with the Monster. Of course, there was damn little money for presents, but there was money for cigarettes and booze. The kids would make paper chains and little gifts for each other. Some years they had a tree, most years they didn't. Christmas seemed to bring out the worst in the Monster. Everyone, including Mary would walk around on egg shells trying to please him and pretend they were happy while really they were waiting and dreading for the Monster to blow. It was a rare Christmas that he didn't.

Over Christmas holidays, Maggie would spend a lot of time upstairs, even though it was cold up there, she would sit and talk to Jennifer, make up poems or play "Gone With The Wind". She would hope that he didn't know where she was and would leave her alone. But, he knew. Just to hear him bellow out her name would put her into a panic, but she would always answer him and go down to obey whatever it was that he wanted of her.

The Monster would make the kids stand in line by age and sing songs and carols for him. He never once went to a school concert to see them perform, but now, he wanted them to perform for him. The children, of course would have to do as they were told, even though they hated it, they would sing for him, knowing that the wrath of the Monster might come down on them.

The saddest part of Christmas was while the rest of the world was rejoicing and celebrating, thinking about "peace on earth and goodwill to all men", the entire family was living in fear and panic and wishing it were over.

The children knew that they could not expect holidays to be happy events. There was very seldom any money and unless their father was in his "happy drunk" role, making jokes that they had to laugh at and food that they had to eat, holidays were not happy times.

9

There was a T. V. in the house from the mid 1950's, and a telephone, a party line, but nevertheless, the children were not allowed to touch either. When the Monster was not at home, Mary would allow the kids to watch the T.V. they would have one ear on tires in the driveway and could have it turned off and had   all vacated the room, taking with them every trace that they were ever in there by the time the door knob turned. But the phone - no, never. If the Monster ever caught us on the phone, there would be hell to pay and it would be Mary who would get it. Of course, we would not even think of it when he was at home, it just didn't enter our minds. As a result, we learned to associate the phone with panic and fear as we associated may ordinary things in life. Some of us, to this day hate talking on the phone and only use it to convey a message, or in an emergency.

We knew that we were being deprived and abused. We hated him and yet we so much needed to be loved and simply acknowledged as human beings. We would do anything to try to gain his approval, to make him notice us, and most of all love us. We would lie to him about anything that might give us a tiny bit of attention, on the other hand, we deeply feared that the attention might be horrible punishment. We were only children, how could we possibly know that his only feelings of fatherhood were feelings of control. As long as he could control us completely, he thought we would feel loved. He saw the control as protection and as long as he had all his little soldiers in line, he could play his part of Commanding Officer.

Secret Storms

Deep in her soul
secret storms are raging
filling her heart
with sadness and despair.
Turmoil goes on and on
lightning crackling
across her mind,
thunder booming
in her ears -
her life unfolding in
garbled thoughts
flashing memories of
nightmares, horrors,
fears of huge powerful monsters
and she is only
a small and helpless child.

~ CHAPTER TWO ~

IN THE BEGINNING

"Discipline is the ingrained   habit of willing, cheerful and unhesitating obedience".
- Old Military response

Let's go back to the beginning. Maggie was born in the spring of 1945 right at the end of the war. Twelve years later the last of the children had been born which made Margaret the second eldest of eight. Her mother, Mary, suffered terribly during those years, not only from the effects of constant pregnancy and child birth but more profoundly from the constant abuse and belittlement from her husband, Ronald. Mary said very little, cried a lot and tried very hard to keep her children and her home together. Back then, (at least in Mary's world,) there were no books on abusive relationships, no birth control pills, no doctors prescribing anti-depressants; if you made your bed, you not only lay in it, you damned well stayed with it for better or worse, or the rules of the universe would have been broken and heaven would be denied.

Her husband didn't believe in birth control, he did believe that when a man wanted sex, he took it. Condoms were the only form of birth control in those days, but he was much too selfish to use them and quite often too drunk to care. He complained constantly of too many mouths to feed, but when asked, he would reply "Well, it's her damn fault, she's knocked up again, too bad for her."

By the age of thirty-five, Mary was tired of her life and looked it. She was very thin from years of giving up her share of food to the hungry children and it was no wonder, her hair was already white. Usually, she tried to force a smile but much of the time, her life was a painful existence. If only she had a washing machine, a bathroom, a hair cut, some money. If only the kids weren't so needy if only, if only. If only she could confide in Granny like little Maggie did. If only she had a friend, if only he wasn't so mean, if only she didn't hate him, if only he would leave her alone at night.

Mary had been the only girl in a family where carrying on the family name was very important. Although her parents were kind to her, she could never remember anyone every being emotional or hugging and in all her life, she couldn't remember her mother ever kissing her. She wanted, no craved that love that she felt she missed as a child, but she knew that she also could not show love to her own children once they were out of infancy, she had simply never learned how. Even if she had, her husband wouldn't allow it. Mary did not have access to books or information that could have told her that the very reasons that her mother craved but could not show love, she craved but could not show love, and so down through the generations, her children would not only learn not to show love, but not to feel any emotion - only fear.

Mary did love her children from the bottom of her heart, she just couldn't show it. She was in so much pain of her own, physically, mentally and emotionally, that there was a constant battle with herself going on in her mind. If Ron said "No", then she had to say "No" even if she knew better, even if she knew he was dead wrong. She also had to lie constantly to try to keep peace especially between the children and their father, or in fact to stop their father from killing them. Something that Mary never even thought of was the fact that she was the only person that her daughters had to look up to and the only person they would have to mold their lives after, just as Mary had become a copy of her own mother.

Years ago, Mary had been happy to have babies and to love them and care for them. When she would see a newborn, her breasts would tingle and she would think of her own babies. Until Ron started drinking, he wasn't the best husband, but he wasn't the Monster he had turned out to be, but Mary's life had become a nightmare. He quite often threatened to kill himself, sometimes Mary half wished he would.

Ronald portrayed a man with great self concept, confidence and self respect. He emanated power over his own life and over the lives of others. He believed that others respected and loved him and that everything he did and said was "right". His "rightness" had to be constantly confirmed.

In Ronald's childhood, his father was quite high up in the military and the family of three boys and a girl lived quite well. Their childhood was happy and although their father was "military strict", they loved and respected him. When Ron was ten, his father died, quite suddenly of pneumonia. Then the Great Depression hit and the investments and insurance company that carried the policy on the life of his dad had gone bankrupt. Ron grew up to be angry and bitter.

He felt that the death of his father meant he had abandoned the family and had left them with nothing.

Nineteen Thirty Nine brought the Second World War and Ronald joined the Air Force. That was how he met Mary, she was also in the Air Force. Ron with a great need for power and Mary feeling lost, far from home and venerable they fulfilled each other's needs. Many military wives are abused because of just that. The military attracts men who are in search of power, the uniform, the prestige and sense of belonging to a great army of power and of course, they seek out women who are in need of strength and have low self esteem. Using the armed forces as a security blanket of power, these men are quite often very good soldiers and take pride in their position in life. A soldier doesn't need to show emotion or love or tenderness. He can be a "Yes Sir, No Sir" robot and to his superiors, as long as he obeys the commands and the rules, he is an excellent soldier. However as husbands and fathers, these men find they cannot relate emotionally and therefore they use their power to control instead of love. Ron became an extremely rigid thinker, unwilling to sway from his preconceived ideas which he defended (drunk or sober) by shouting in order to intimidate the poor soul who might attempt to defy him. He refused to listen or to accept any explanation or to discuss any topic that might encourage free thinking. He was a prejudiced man in politics, religion, race and sex, believing that only his beliefs were correct, he demanded it. He was a dictator who constantly demanded conformity and submission especially in his wife and children. He also demanded that they humor him with constant praise, he would ask for praise by saying things like, "I am a great man, aren't I Mary? Yes, of course I am everyone respects me and loves me".

In reality he was an alcoholic, who had to constantly feed his own pride but was unable to feed his own children. True to his addiction, somehow he had the money for booze and cigarettes.

Of course, he was never wrong and therefore had to place blame and guilt on others to prove himself right. He idolized the military, war and weapons, glorifying each and constantly recounting the same war stories over and over again until his wife and children were fed up to the teeth with it. He always went on about what he had to give up in his life and never seemed to care that his children were doing without proper food, doctors, dentists, clothes, books for school, toilet paper, feminine products, toothpaste, soap, deodorant etc. etc..

The Monster's most famous saying was "discipline is the ingrained habit of willing, cheerful and unhesitating obedience ." We all learned not to think, only to obey. "Unhesitating obedience" became a comfort zone for Mary and then, for her children. They became good and obedient wives, good and obedient employees, good and obedient mothers. They needed to be told, they could not function without being told. As long as they were being told what to do, they could go about life with some amount of comfort in that they didn't have to accept any blame. After all, they were always told what to do. In trying to define "unhesitating obedience" try to picture a robot, or a person who has been so brainwashed that she obeys blindly, without thinking. If it is demanded that a person obey without thinking, then it is demanded that she not think at all.

Whenever the children did not live up to their father's expectations, he would blame it on inherited traits from their mother's family. If they cried or showed any "weakness" at all, it was a fault inherited from Mary. He spoke of Mary's "people" with complete disrespect as though they were all idiots. This of course was not true. The sad part is that the children had to believe what they were told. It hurt Mary to the core. Of course, she didn't realize that he was doing it to feed off the power trip high it gave him, and yes, he meant to hurt her.

Life was a hard battle. In order to survive, Mary and the children learned to obey without reasoning. They all learned not to think, only to do as they were told, and in their quest for a sense of self, they never got beyond the basic needs level of existence, their needs then were very simple, not praying for love or wealth, but asking God only for food and shoes.

Don't think, just obey.
Don't ever reason, or ask why.
Don't show any emotion and
Don't you ever cry.

Don't be a real person,
Don't feel hate or pain.
Don't ask the Lord for sympathy
just shelter from the rain.

~ CHAPTER THREE ~

HER OWN TRUE LOVE

"Be mine forever, my own true love" *the theme from* *Gone With the Wind.*

At the age of fourteen, Maggie had grown into a lovely young woman. She had learned at school that to the best of her ability, she must keep herself clean. Although there was no running water in the house, no bathroom or toilet and all water must be carried in and carried out, Maggie and her older sister Jane started bathing every Saturday, washing each other's hair, and caring about their looks. The petty jealousies of their younger life seemed to be disappearing. They managed this weekly bathing, as on Saturdays, Ron was always at the Legion. They thought that if he were around, they wouldn't be allowed and they didn't want to find out. The girls were not allowed to wear makeup of any kind. They were not allowed bras or stockings. They were not allowed to shape their nails or wear their hair down. The sisters had finally become friends.

Jennifer and Maggie, on the other hand, seemed to be constantly at each other's throat . It was getting hard to believe that they had been such close friends. Jennifer didn't like the way that Maggie was constantly lying to people just for attention or to get praise. Then one day they had a terrible argument. Who the hell did Jenny think she was telling Maggie that she couldn't smoke. Maggie told Jenny to get out of her life and stay out. Anyway, they split up. Jenny simply disappeared and Maggie fell secretly in love with a man who lived close by. He was five years older, finished high school and all. She promised herself that she wouldn't tell a soul.

Just like Scarlet O'Hara, her own true love was not to be. As nothing in her life had ever been really real, she kept her love a secret tucked deep within her heart fantasizing constantly and living for each moment she would see him even from across the street. She loved him so deeply that just to say his name took her breath away. Then, like all the other girls her age, she found a boy friend. Her feelings for her boyfriend were a copy of what all the other girls would say about feelings for their boyfriends which had nothing to do with her real, true, pure love.

In order to escape the harsh realities of their lives, children who are abused quite often learn to live within their imagination. The trauma that they have suffered causes them to use the defenses of disassociation and fantasy to keep them alive and sane. In their minds, they carry on a constant chatter with themselves, playing all parts in a stage production that is their life. How clearly they think in the real world depends on how deeply they are living in their imagination. Quite often, at school for instance, they cannot focus on what is going on in the classroom, because in their heads they are miles away, all the time. The only way to keep the pain under control is to stay in the imagination. They speak only when spoken to and then they are quiet and shy. Their shyness is actually fear. Many of these children are termed "backward", when the reality is that they quite often have above average intelligence. By living in the imagination, the child can escape and forget about the horrors in their lives, but the world within the imagination is not by any means real and they find it hard to relate to the real world.   By the time she got to high school, Maggie was lost. She feared everything, teachers, other students, getting lost, not being able to open her locker. So that she wouldn't have to face these fears, she lived more and more in her imagination, and as a result, her school work suffered.   She didn't seem to want to grasp what was being taught. When teachers would send a note home to her parents, there would be no reply.   Their calls went unanswered.   In fact her parents never once attended a parent, teacher interview, or showed any interest whatsoever in her school work. At school, the teachers of course had no understanding of what was going on.

At sixteen, Maggie's drunken father told her to "get out", of course she did as she was told, but she was totally unprepared for what the world had in store for her and because she had been so controlled,   and was so much into her own mind, facing the world alone was nowhere near what she had imagined and even harder than the nightmare she lived at home.

~ CHAPTER FOUR ~

AROUND AND AROUND

I could not love him because he could not love me.
I could not feel his touch and I would not return it.
His body became grotesque for
he could not find beauty in mine.
I dared not respect him because his respect for me
was false for I was unworthy of respect because
I did not love him.
He could not understand me,
I could not be understood
by a man I could not understand.
I watched him suffocate,
he watched me suffocate, strangled by familiarity.
We could not grow together because
neither was growing - we parted.
I was sad that he was sad that I was sad that
suffocating together is easy, growing apart is sad.
Our children cried,
but he could not love me because
I could not love him.

At the age of eighteen, Maggie was married to her boyfriend and had a son. Although she wasn't unhappy, she wasn't happy either. Most of the logic in life was still coming from her imagination. Sex consisted of him kissing her once or twice, mounting her and a couple of minutes later she would think "thank God it is over". She didn't know what was wrong with this scene, but somehow it wasn't right.   What kept her believing in romance was her constant day dreaming about her "own true love". Somehow through the years, she kept her own true love a secret. It was so delicious just to leave it at that. After ten years, and another son, her husband left her and she let him go. She didn't hate him, she just didn't love him. He could not fit into her dreams.

She spent a year alone which was hard. She was forced to make decisions for herself and take care of herself as well as the two boys. She worked every day, housework and kids at night, still imagining that one day her own true love would come and take her away.

Then she met Gary. Gary was good looking had money and a good job. He was also a very kind and loving person. Maggie thought she loved him but she didn't know or realize she was totally incapable of real adult love. In her imagination, she was still saving herself for her soul mate, her own true love.

She and Gary "moved in" together. 'Though their relationship was not perfect, sex was good, food was good and a father for two growing boys was definitely good. They stayed together for twelve years. By this time her youngest was eighteen. Maggie had started to understand that if she was ever going to be happy, she needed to go back and reclaim her childhood. She read every book she could get her hands on and watched every T.V. program. Gary couldn't understand her. Being raised in a close, loving, farm family, he couldn't feel her pain. She was bright, good looking, but deeply disturbed. He let her go.

Then, Maggie's father died. This broke her heart, not because she loved him, she didn't, she hated him, but because he had the nerve to die without ever even saying one loving or tender word to her; without even talking about her childhood and why she hated him; without even one small apology from him, one hug, one small kiss on the forehead. How dare that bastard die without even talking to her, without even validating her life. Depression that had plagued her since childhood returned with a vengeance. She suffered migraine headaches, agoraphobia, and panic attacks. She drank more, smoked more until her life became one huge hangover - as you learn, so you become.

Then to top it all off, Maggie met the younger version of her father - Mark. He was a loud, obnoxious demanding, abusing son of a bitch who treated her like a door mat. Of course, she married him.

Over the years, Maggie and Jenny seldom spoke. The odd time, Maggie would, through her drunken tears call out for Jenny, but they had grown worlds apart.

Mark's first wife, Beth had left him for another man, and left her two little girls with Mark. A few months later, after Mark and Maggie had settled into a not too blissful relationship, Beth wanted Mark back and set out to get him. While Mark Maggie were away for a weekend, Beth moved back into the house. She was willing to play every trick in the book. Maggie fought tooth and nail hang on to her man. She had no idea why, wasn't that what she was supposed to do? Maggie didn't know, so she would just have another beer and think about it in the morning. Maggie and Mark moved into Maggie's old apartment.

This story gets even more sick.

Beth called Mark over to the house, got Mark

good and drunk and she seduced him knowing it was her fertile time. Next step of course was to tell everyone in her world that she was pregnant with Mark's child. Beth knew that Mark would move back with her as the prospect of having a son totally thrilled him. About two weeks later, Mark again went to the house to find her gone. She wasn't pregnant after all and had taken off back to her boyfriend leaving Mark and Maggie with their relationship dangling and two little girls to take care of.

Mark's girls had the same love/hate relationship with their father as Maggie had with her own father. Although Maggie could relate to this, she found she was becoming more and more numb to it and of course, if she did not support Mark in his opinions and decisions, he would make her sorry that she even thought of it.

Maggie's life sunk lower and lower into the deep ditch of depression. She would get up early in the morning, drink her coffee, smoke several cigarettes, take her pain pills, pray for relief from her hangover, get ready and go to work. At dinnertime, she would walk home, have a beer and several cigarettes for lunch, suck on cough lozenges to take away the smell of the beer and go back to work. She returned home at five and made supper. By nine o'clock, she was sufficiently medicated to sleep and so life went on day after day, year after year.

Mark's girls had lived most of their lives on the same street. Two doors down lived a single mom and three kids. The dad was in jail and the two girls and one boy spent a great deal of time down at Mark's. When sober enough, Maggie would help all the kids with their homework and tried to be a friend to them. Shelley, the oldest would watch Maggie paint and seemed to take an interest in art so Maggie tried to encourage her.

All summer long the five kids would be making up plays and having endless games of Monopoly, playing tapes and dancing, the same type of summer games all kids enjoyed. There were always kids sleeping over.

One night Maggie had made Shelley, then eleven, a bed on the sofa and said good night. Mark of course, as always, was drunk. The next morning Maggie got up at six as usual and noticed that Shelley had gone. You guessed it, Mark had molested her. Mark didn't even deny it, claiming that he was drunk and blaming Maggie because he wasn't getting enough sex so, of course he had to turn to others and therefore it was all Maggie's fault. He even accused her of not being responsible for children sleeping over, and refused to accept any blame. It was Maggie who felt the shame, guilt and remorse, and Maggie who called Shelley's mother and through her sobs and tears apologized for Mike's drunken behavior.

Shelley had no idea at the time that she would eventually be Mark's live in doormat and would have a child with him. Even just after accusing Mark, Shelley was still spending most of her free time at the house. As time went by, she had grown into an extremely overweight teenager with huge breasts. Maggie became suspect when Mark and Shelley were spending a lot of time alone together and Mark was buying Shelley things, like loaded sodas. More on Shelley later.

Shame

Shame is harsh ugly words
 and angry cursings.
Shame is threats and bruises
 and shattering glass.
Shame is a scream in the night
 and the cry of a child.

Shame is blood on a towel
 and a black eye in the morning.
Shame is empty beer bottles,
a hangover, an overturned chair.
Shame is reaching out,
crying out, screaming for anyone to help.

Shame is confession and remorse.
Shame is telling,
being heard and understanding.
Shame is vowing never again
- until the next time:

- and people will say "what a shame".

One summer evening, Mark's two daughters had gone to visit their mother for the weekend, all hell broke loose and the neighbors again called 911. Again the police answered the "domestic". Again Mark had threatened her life and again Maggie sat sobbing and mumbling about how he had a knife. Again, Mark had left, again Maggie would not lay charges. On the following day, Maggie answered a knock at the door. There stood a lady in full police uniform carrying a clip board and asking if she could come in. She was from "Victim Services" and told Maggie that if she didn't get out, one day they would be carrying her out in a body bag. "I have seen this over and over again," she said. "It never gets better, only worse." She gave Maggie a pamphlet on how the government spends millions of dollars a year on family violence and police investigations which end in either the wife won't lay charges, or the wife spends a few days in the "shelter"and then returns to the abuser. She also gave Maggie a paper explaining family violence; not only wife abuse, but violence against children, elderly people, family members and even animals. It went on to explain that the abuser is mentally ill and needs medical and psychological help and that the partner as co-dependent quite often doesn't realize that she is making matters worse by staying. The children would likely grow up to be abusers or victims themselves and so family violence continues down the generations. It also gave startling facts and statistics on how many lives one violent man addicted to alcohol or drugs could ruin.

Victim Services had set up an appointment with a councillor in a group for abused women. She insisted that Maggie go and even though she was depressed and confused, she was still obedient so Maggie went. Within the group, Maggie learned many things about abuse. To her surprise, the group was always full and there was a waiting list.

Mark did all he could to discourage her. He

yelled and stormed and drank himself stupid, but every Wednesday after supper, Maggie went to a place of safety and insight and caring.

Maggie was still so sure that she could change Mark. She still felt that deep down he was a good person and sooner or later he would understand that if he loves her, he must change for her. But, no one changes for someone else, he could only change for himself.   If Maggie was upset or trying to explain her feelings, Mark would tell Maggie to give her head a shake, that she was insane, that she imagined things. Maggie had so little esteem, so little confidence in herself that she couldn't deny that quite often she lived in her imagination, that maybe she was insane.   Mark refused to even acknowledge that there was a problem, and if there was, it was hers.. One statement made by the counselor that stays in Maggie's mind to this day is "you can usually tell what his future behavior will be, just look at his past behavior."

The counselor helped Maggie to make a plan of escape. She showed her ways of hiding away a few dollars at a time and how to pack an emergency get away bag, what to take and what to leave behind. She also told her that the most important thing to get away with was her life.

A few days later, Maggie sat down at the computer and set out in search of her old childhood friend.

~CHAPTER FIVE ~

REMINDERS

Emotions emerge from
the dark depths of our memories.
Powerful scenes locked away
in the black cellars of our minds
now surface and take us by surprise.
Thoughts and dreams long forgotten,
fears of childhood days gone by
now vivid reminders of our dark secrets
pushed and forced down the cellar hatch
but now the door won't close,
and sometimes we have to face
those desperate emotions that still live
within the dark core of our souls.

September 10, 1998

Dear Jennifer,

I am fifty two years old and I am still searching desperately for some meaning in my life. Please help me. I hate myself for what I have become, I can't even face myself in the mirror. If I ever needed you, I need you now - please Jen don't leave me in this pit.

I am so depressed, I start drinking at about ten in the morning and I drink thru until I go to bed around 9 or 10. I smoke over a pack a day. I feel like I belong in the gutter. When you watch T.V. and see those street people so lost and dirty, searching and begging for anything that will take away the pain for a little while, that's me. That is how I feel . I am either so depressed or, so drunk, I can't even focus my thoughts, I don't want to. I just want to go somewhere where it won't hurt anymore.

The counselor told me that if I want my life to get better, I would have to face and admit the truth, follow the steps, walk thru the pain, pick up the pieces and start over. She gave me a sheet of what I need to do to find peace. Reading it at first, I really couldn't relate to it, but the more I think on it, the more I need it. Here is a list of the main points. I didn't write down all of it, but it should give you the main drift.

1. Admit to yourself that you have had enough pain, that you want to change your life.

2. Make a list of positive affirmations confirming what you want in life and repeat them several times a day.

3. Take ownership of and responsibility for everything that has happened to you and every emotion you have felt from your age of rebellion (say 16) on.

4. You have to be willing to go through the pain to get to the other side.

5. Make a list of all the beliefs you can think of that you have carried since childhood and how they have changed to what they are today.

6. Write a letter to each and every person that has hurt you or done you wrong in your life and tell each that you forgive them.

7. Get into and stay in the here and now. Remember, what is, is and what ain't, ain't.

8. By your attitude and the way you treat others, show others how to treat you, show them how you want

to be treated.

9. How will you know if you are healing? You will know, it will occur to you that you are becoming more and more a Survivor and less and less a Victim. Get a notebook and write down every time it occurs to you that are doing, thinking, feeling, is a direct result of your childhood.

~~~~~~~~

I am going to try with all my heart to follow those steps. I have to get out of here, I really do, but where would I go, what would I do? I have no money. Anyway, no matter where I go or what I do, all the garbage and hate from my past is still with me, the Monster is still with me. I cannot deny the Monster. And then, there is Mark. How can I leave him? His has a big drinking problem and he is so helpless. He doesn't mean to hurt me, or yell at me. He has to go into a rage - he is just letting off steam. When he goes off the deep end, I should learn to keep my mouth shut. If I didn't defend myself, he would probably shut up. Plus, if I leave, how will he make the mortgage payment. That means we would loose the house and I would loose all that I have worked for and payed for all these years. Anyway he told me that if I leave, he will kill me, but I know that if I stay, eventually he will kill me anyway. The worst part of that thought is that I just don't care anymore. God help me.

Love Maggie

Defeat

Cry, beg, surrender;
turn, run and hide.
Think of words like courage,
strength and fortitude.
Show him that
you are determined
to be a person,
to stand alone.
Try to stop yourself
no! no panic,
no fear of the unknown.
He speaks to you,
demands of you
draining your strength,
numbing your mind -
crushing your soul;
then you return home,
you return to him
and know
that you are defeated.

December 2, 1998

Dear Jennifer,

      I left him again last Thursday and went back on Sunday. I went to my sister's and drank a lot of beer. He called and threatened me again so, I went home. I am so afraid. Afraid that Mark will hurt someone and I can't be responsible for what might happen.

      He has been hiding his quite active sexual

relationship with Shelley because she is only fifteen and he knows that he could go to jail for it. He is so afraid that I know what is going on that he is promising me that he will change and is on his best behavior. He spends a great deal of time at Shelley's house. Her father is now out of jail and living at home, so Marv and Mark are good friends. I wonder what will happen when Marv finds out that his good friend, Mark is doing his daughter. Dear God, Jen, this is sick, where can I find the strength to get out of here. Why do I sit here day after day feeling sorry for myself? I know I have to go, why can't I find the courage to do it?

I know, I know, I have to face reality. I have done the "group", been for counseling, read all the books and seen all the T.V. shows and how much better is the marriage how much better is my life? What that cop told me is true he will kill me and I can just hear him say "I didn't mean it, I loved her." I think I will go back out to the Island. I love it there, Chris is there, he will take care of me I just have to go and start over. I will put my air fare on the first card that pops out of my wallet and go. If I can only make that first step, maybe the rest will fall into place for me. Maybe my life will become a happy life instead of constantly miserable . It is so hard for me to understand that it is my choice, it is up to me how I want to live. Everything I have done in my life has always seemed to be against me, everything is such a struggle and I keep doing the wrong thing over and over again. This is what I am afraid of, I mean, if I try to stand on my own two feet, I will probably fall flat on my face. I don't know how much falling down and getting up I can take. But, I will just have to keep trying. If I fall on my face, I will just have to get up, brush myself off and start over. Stay with me girl, I am gaining courage.

Love, Maggie.

1. Admit to yourself that you have had enough, that you want to change. Make that statement - period. No yea but I don't have a job, or yea but what about the kids, or any other excuse you can come up with NOT to take your own life into your own hands and do something positive. That includes getting out of any abusive relationship and giving up any crutches or medications ie. booze, drugs, food, gambling or whatever else you may be addicted to.

P. S. I bought the ticket, I am leaving on Thursday. The gal from Victim Services has offered to drive me to the Airport. I am scared, so scared!

Keep putting one foot ahead of the other,
go on from day to day.
Keep thinking " I can do this."
No, there is no other way.
Don't listen to the evil voices,
Keep saying in your mind
"God help me, I can do this,
I can leave hell behind" -
and keep walking.

~CHAPTER SIX~

LOST

If I am lost in the woods,
where am I?

Am I still here,
still part of the Universe?

If I am lost in the woods,
I am only lost because I think I am.

But, if my soul is lost
where am I?

If I cannot find myself
then am I truly lost?

January 14, 1999

Dear Jennifer,

Happy New Year. I am sober, cold, hungry and depressed. I had put my first and last month's rent on a little apartment using the same card that my airline ticket had been charged to and now I don't have money to make a payment. The plan to live with my son and have him take care of me didn't happen. Why do I always need someone to take care of me, to tell me what to do and look after me - so I don't have to be responsible for my own life and can't blame myself for the outcome? Exactly. I am still afraid of falling on my face. I stayed with Chris and Janet for three weeks, and I had a strong feeling that I was intruding on their lives, plus they didn't want me smoking around the kids and I don't blame them. I dial the job line every morning and have applied for every position that I thought I could handle, - nothing. I am sure that the lady at the Unemployment office thinks "Oh God, here she comes again".   The fact is it takes every ounce of courage I have to force myself to open that door and walk in. It takes even more courage to even speak to someone. My problem is that I am so down on myself that prospective employers would see the lack of self confidence right away. I know that, but self confidence isn't something I can fake, I just plain don't have any.

As a child, I went hungry over and over again. Now, at my age, after working so hard for all these years, to go hungry somehow doesn't seem right. Now I almost feel that at my age I have earned the right not to go hungry. Damn it, do I have to beg? I don't know what to do, there is no-one to tell me what to do.   I feel so lost, the panic goes on and on.

This town is cold in January. As I walked down town, the wind whipped snow into my face and I thought about what it would be like to freeze to death. I had read a book when I was young about a girl who is walking thru a snow storm and finds she just can't go on.   She simply lies down in the ditch and lets the angels take her away. Back to reality.   I walked down to Water Street and turned into the National Bank building. Just inside the door, that familiar pounding of my heart and spinning feeling backed me against a wall.

I went back outside and lit a cigarette, waiting until the panic attack passed. I   followed the signs to the basement and found the door to the Family and Social Services, - the welfare office.

I noticed my hand was shaking as I took the clipboard and pen from the girl behind the desk.. I tried to avoid her eyes, I felt so ashamed. The form asked all the pertinent questions. How much money do I have in the bank? Am I expecting a windfall? Ha! Ha!. I glanced around the room at the toy box in the corner, copies of Women's Day and Better Homes on the end table and in the corner sat a dirty, bearded old man. He kept sniffing of snot back up his nose and looking at me. ' Oh dear God,' I thought, 'what has my life come to? Where is the joy in living, the peace, where is the peace?' I thought of a song we sang in Sunday School all those years ago - "All things bright and beautiful, all creatures great and small, all things wise and wonderful, the Lord God made them all. " Where dear God, where is bright and beautiful? The girl behind the desk called "Margaret". I got up and followed her down a maze of hallways and into a small room.

A man with a nice smile - nice teeth stood and shook my hand. "Sit down" he motioned to a chair across from his desk. He reviewed the clip-board and looked directly at me. "Well, we can't help you here, my dear. You have your final month's rent paid, you still have two "unemployment checks" coming. I understand that your son is working and must be quite able to support you. The nice smile re-appeared and he waited for me to speak. I couldn't, if I did, the big lump in my throat would have let go. All I wanted was comfort. I just needed to know that someone cared and that if I did use up my last month's rent, there was someone I could go to who would know that I had tried so hard to find work and that I needed a little help to get on my feet.

"You do have a husband, Mrs. eh - - "? He glanced down again at the clipboard for my name. " Where is he? - I see, had a little spat? Well, I would suggest you kiss and make up. Your life would be a lot easier that way. Sometimes marital problems can get blown out of proportion, don't you agree?"

That smile again. I felt like screaming at him , but I didn't say a word. If I had said anything, I would have cried and crying is not allowed. I didn't dare look at him again. I simply got up, walked out. The late afternoon sun was slowly fading and the cold wind whipped mercilessly. I kept walking, with the wind blowing in my face, no-one could see the tears.

Pain, it's about embracing pain, realizing that pain is human and to be human there must be pain. Even in my imagination, I still can't make that pain go away.

I realize that I am not alone in my suffering, there is no such thing as a perfect life, everyone is suffering to some degree or another. Although I desperately wanted someone to care, of course I couldn't tell my secrets, that would mean that people would know what a horrible person I was and I would be breaking the promise I made to myself as a child. - On the way home I picked up a pack of cigarettes and twelve beer. To hell with food.

~CHAPTER SEVEN ~

AGAINST THE WIND

When the wind is calm and quiet
if I listen just at dusk
I can hear the birds
quietly chirping to their babies
singing a lullaby as the day ends
and the wind is still.
When the wind is calm and quiet
I can hear the church bell from a mile away
peeling out a mass, a birth,
a death, a wedding,
beautiful clear still chimes in God's name
when the wind is still.
When the wind is calm and quiet
I can hear the crunching
of my feet along the sidewalk,
see my life's breath in puffs of fresh steam
feel my pulse, hear my heartbeat
when the wind is still.
When the wind is calm and quiet
I can hear the sweet young voices
of children in the park chasing,
playing, running
with the bursting energy of youth
in a game they will live forever
when the wind is still.

But -
When the wind is lashing in from the sea,
whipping, smashing, pushing
the cold salt spray against my face
as though the anger of the world
were behind it -
assaulting my very soul
when the wind is wild.
When the wind is howling through the trees,
smacking, cracking branches,
shoving mother nature
into places she does not want to be,
then so harshly
lashing again and again
when the wind is wild.
When the wind is swirling, whistling
it is filling up my mind,
so that I cannot hear
the gentle beautiful side of life
only the wrath
of the wild, wild wind.

February 11, 1999

Dear Jennifer,

     If only I could find a job, I know I would be O.K.. Yes, I am REALLY depressed and REALLY broke. If I were working, I would at least be relating to other people and I would have a reason to get up in the morning.   I don't know how far down in this pitiful pit I still have to go to hit bottom. I have quit drinking not because I had to or because I wanted to. It took no will power at all, the simple fact is I have no money. Quitting did take a lot of nightmare type thoughts, thoughts of going back, thoughts of begging, thoughts that I can't do this. The old saying "One day at a time" doesn't apply to me, I can't even hack five minutes at a time.

I also have no furniture. Chris got me a bed from relatives and the rest I make do with overturned boxes, an old plastic table and two patio chairs. I still have my little black and white T.V., but I have no money coming in and I can't pay the rent.

It seems as if I am afraid of the dark and the whole world is black. I'll write later.

Love, Maggie

"My personal trials have taught me the value of unmerited suffering. As my sufferings mounted, I soon realized that there were two ways that I could respond to my situation: either to react with bitterness or seek to transform the suffering into a creative force."

Martin Luther King

March 12, 1999

Dear Jennie,

The move to a slum apartment in a slum building has taught me a lot about how really rough the world is! I haven't eaten meat in weeks. I am so sick of those packages of just add boiling water noodles, they can go

41

a long way if you eat small servings, but especially at night I have cravings for real food.   I go into the food bank and get day old bread or buns, and dip it into the noodles. The food bank is only about a mile to walk but in the cold it feels like ten.

On my little T.V., without cable I can only get two channels, on Sunday afternoons there is a show that always starts the same way.   The camera picks up several skinny, sad African children and the announcer sais "...Without your help, many of these children will go to bed hungry - stay with us and we will let you know how you can help." Every time I see this I could scream. Why don't they show hungry people in our own cities, in our own country, many of who go to bed hungry every night and can't afford necessities in life like prescriptions and toilet paper - like me.

I really miss my car, especially here. There are no busses at all so I either have to walk or take a cab. I have always hated driving, because I have always had such fear about it. Now, what I would give to have a car. I'm not saying that the fear would disappear, but I could always take it slow or be a fair weather driver.

Walking everywhere can be the total pits in the winter. For a cab, uptown and back it costs eight dollars. That is a lot of money, money I need for food.

Yes, being a true nicotine addict I still buy tobacco and roll and smoke those suckers one after the other.

For all the years that I lived with, and off the men in my life I never realized that it is so hard just to feed myself.   I have called Mark several times and his answering machine is always on. So far, he hasn't called me back. Maybe God is taking care of me, cause if he did call, at this point, I would probably go back to him. Now that is a laugh, I have a restraining order so that he can't hurt me and I am thinking of going back to him. I am depressed and hungry, I don't know what I am thinking.

This building has also taught me a lot about what happens in some lives. Last week there was a stabbing in the hall over drugs. The guy who was stabbed and bleeding was delirious and tried to break my door down to get out. I was so scared, I thought my heart would jump out of my chest.

The walls are made of two by two's and gyprock. My bed is next to the wall that adjoins someone else's bedroom. The other night I could hear the sounds of people making love so clearly that I could hear every breath. It made me feel sick to my stomach, I pulled a pillow over my ears. It suddenly dawned on me that what I was hearing was two men making love - welcome to the real world, Maggie.

The rats and mice in this building are unbelievable. I got two big boxes of rat poison and they have eaten it all and just keep coming and coming. It seems that the more I feed them poison, they go and tell all their friends where to go for a good meal before they die. I keep all of my food, which is precious little, in the fridge because the fridge is the only cupboard that they can't get into.   I hate it at night, I can hear them in the walls and in the attic they scurry and fight or maybe they are not fighting, maybe they are making thousands of babies to replace the ones that I poison. Sometimes I dream that they are crawling on me. I wake up so scared that I can't get back to sleep. Maybe that's why I sleep so much in the daytime. The critters also die in the walls and the stink would drive a pig out of the barn.

When I told the landlord, he shrugged and said "that's nothing". Well it is something and I hate it! In my whole life so far, I have never even thought about living with rats.

Love, Maggie

I know how to reach into my soul
and turn off the switch called pain.
Once the switch is off
I can pretend that I am human,
pretend that I can walk down the street,
talk to people, and live without panic.
But somehow down deep in my soul,
something clicks, the world goes dark
and I know it is the switch is on
and I must suffer again.

March 23, 1999

Dear Jennie,

I have had a terrible tooth ache. It throbs and throbs. It gets so bad, I cry. Don't even think of it, no money, no dentist. After the third day, there was swelling along my jaw and I could feel the infection all the way down my neck. It must have abscessed, it had to come out. I took the needle nosed plyers and a bottle of hydrogen peroxide and prepared (in front of the mirror) to pull the tooth. Every time I would count to three, I would open my eyes and chicken out. Finally I put the pliers around the tooth and left the mirror. Still walking away, with all my might, I yanked on the tooth - hard. I heard a loud "crunch". What I had managed to do was to break it off at the gum line, but I had also broken the abscess. That has to be the most rotten stuff that I have ever tasted. I kept spitting and rinsing several times a day for about a week, the pain slowly went away and the swelling subsided.

I just sunk further and further into the ditch of depression. So much so that I don't want to go anywhere, do anything or speak to anyone. I just want to sleep my life away in my own little world. I would never kill myself. I don't have enough guts. I remember through a flood of tears telling my father that I wanted to die and he told me to shut up, that I didn't have enough guts or brains to kill myself, and that if I tried, I would probably fail because that is how stupid I am.

I sleep the days away. This has some rewards, I can't smoke as many of the cigarettes that I can't afford because I am asleep, and at least when I am dreaming, I am out of this rotten hole, and maybe, just maybe I can dream of my own true love. Or, maybe I am using sleep the way I was using booze, as a way to stay out of the real world, because the real world hurts too much. There are rats in the real world, rats and monsters.

Being depressed is like falling into a deep ditch full of black slime. You try to climb out but you can't get any footing and there are no hand holds and if someone tries to extend a hand to you, you can't see it in the swirling fog that rises constantly from the slime so that you are always disoriented and no matter how hard you try you cannot focus. I do understand about depression and I know there is help out there. I have read several books about it. It has nothing to do with being crazy, or not being able to handle life, it is a chemical imbalance in the brain that can be set right with anti-depressant drugs.

I walked up to the Medical Center today to try and get a doctor to help me, to do something, anything, perhaps ask for some sample anti-depressant medication, but the doctor on duty said he didn't have any samples so he gave me a prescription. I was too ashamed to tell him I had no money. Then, I had to walk all the way back down-town against the March wind. Part way home I thought hold it, hold it. Why am I doing this. All I am doing is feeling sorry for myself, but I am not really willing to help myself, if I were, I would have told the doctor that I have no money. Just tell the truth, that's all I have to do. I don't have to feel ashamed. Telling the truth is so hard for an abuse victim. It is almost as if everything will go away or it won't hurt as long as no one knows the truth. Or, if the world knew, if people could see into my past, my mind, my soul, I would be exposed as the ugly deformed human being that my childhood has made me, so I have to hide it.

The only way I am going to get help is either win a lottery, or tell the truth. I will simply have to tell the truth - better odds.

I turned around and walked back to the clinic, waited another hour and then with a deep breath told the doctor that I was broke - and depressed. He smiled knowingly, and gave me a sample pack of medication and then told me to make an appointment with his office for next week. Why, oh why couldn't I have done that months, no years ago.   Telling the truth is so hard. A big part of my thinking has always been "don't ever tell, don't ever shame yourself or admit anything is wrong in your life."   I am glad I went back, and I got a doctor. Finding a doctor is impossible in this town.

O.K. I took step number one, I got out, I left my husband, my home, car, furniture, all the little treasures I had collected over the years. All of my memories of how I would be happy and grow a garden and plant roses that would bloom forever. All of my dreams have now been reduced to the cold hard facts of reality. Reality hurts and my life certainly isn't much better. No he can't hurt me any more, but I am hurting. It sure is taking a long time for the medication to work!

I know Jennie, if I think depressing thoughts, I will be depressed. If I think happy thoughts, I will be happy, but right now, happy just won't come for me.

P.S.   Maybe I am not as depressed as I thought, I am writing and not sleeping.   That is at least something, isn't it? Do you think I should try step two? Love, Maggie

Take your purpose in life, attach it to a star and never lose it. If you lose it, you have lost your enthusiasm; you have settled for something less. Do not settle for second best, fight like hell for your purpose and your dream and get it." Guru RHH

~ CHAPTER EIGHT~

AFFIRMATIONS

"Belief consists of accepting the affirmations of the soul; disbelief is in denying them".
Ralph Waldo Emerson

2. Make a list of affirmations. This should be a list of what you want to be, ie: I am at peace with my world. I have earned the right to be kind to myself; etc. etc. Every morning when you first wake up, read them out loud to yourself. As you read them, feel the emotion and the impact of each. If you share your life and space with others and you find this difficult, keep your list hidden in the bathroom and read it with the shower running, or find some other private place. Just as you learned by rote as a child to be negative about yourself, so you will learn by rote to replace the negatives with positives. For most people this takes at least a month. Actually, what you are doing by repeating your affirmations, is re-programming your sub-conscious by repetition. Just as you learned, by repetition, so you will unlearn. How many people do you know who, when asked "How are you?" answer with a long list of all their ailments, or with "Oh, not too bad", well how bad is bad? In other words they feel rotten. If they were to practice saying "I feel great", EVERY TIME they are asked, it won't take long until they have learned to feel great. Ask yourself several times a day "How are you?" and answer yourself "I feel great". Make a mental note that you are responding automatically, whether you feel great or not. Soon you will be.

There is no such person as superwoman. There are only millions of women who have chosen to do super things in their lives. Instead of living a life filled with despair, they have chosen to live a life filled with joy and contentment now it is your choice, which will it be?

May 2, 1999

Dear Jennifer,

If it doesn't work, so what, it sure isn't hurting me and God knows I have the time. I have absolutely nothing to loose. In my research, I have done some reading on imprinting. Just as when I was a child, it was imprinted in our brains that we were idiots, incapable of thought, unlovable, etc. etc., then it can also be imprinted in our brains that we are smart, free thinking and lovable which would be the total reverse of what we were first taught. Once we realize that what we were first taught was totally false, only then can we start working on imprinting good thoughts. As I read the affirmations, I try to envision myself and to feel the emotion involved in being a person who, in her own right is valid, working, and earning sufficient money to satisfy her needs. This person feels a wonderful inner glow of peace and serenity in her life and she does not need to drink or smoke to feel that way. When I first thought "envisionment of affirmations" I thought there is no problem envisioning money, or a car, or good food, or being sober, but how do I envision a sense of peace or serenity or contentment. I am pretty sure that it means you have to feel that way as you are repeating your affirmations. Just take a deep breath and envision the feelings as you read out loud. This is what I am going to repeat every morning and every night for at least a month. Then, I may want to add to it, or subtract from it or write a whole new list. Here is my first list:

1. I am still standing, still strong. I am a valid and unique human being.

2. I deserve to find work , to live without hunger, to have money and to enjoy a better standard of living and better life.

3. I feel a wonderful sense of peace within me that keeps me confident and calm.

4. I have the quiet ambiance of being a winner in life.

5.   I do not smoke or drink. I do not need tobacco or alcohol or any other substance in my body. I refuse to become addicted to any substance ever again.

One thing I should not have done, that was to tell the lady who lives down the hall about my affirmations. She thinks I am nuts. She asked me how I could get better if I was constantly lying to myself. I thought about that for a while, but I am going to continue and see how it works. I will not mention it to anyone else.

I went to the library on Sunday and found all kinds of stuff on the Internet. Some of it explains to me why I am the way I am. I am not surprised the learn that millions of people out there are in exactly the same ditch of depression I am in and for the same reasons. Also, I have learned to listen to myself, I am so negative about everything. Every time something goes wrong I call my self a stupid bitch or an ass hole. The same names I hated to hear from the Monster. I learned that the Monster repeatedly calling me names programmed my computer into believing him. The father that I hated has filled me full of hate and negative thoughts.   I see now that I have been programming my computer with all this poor, poor, pitiful me stuff. I have learned that people who have a low self esteem carry the poor, poor, pitiful me thing to the limit. We haven't had the strength to stand up for ourselves, the conditions of our lives, how we live, where we work, how we are treated by people around us, it has been determined by others. This makes us feel inadequate, unable to make decisions for ourselves and anxious because if we try to take control of our lives, what if we fail?   We have handicapped ourselves in our own decision making because we are so afraid to make a mistake. We lie a lot to cover up the truth, name-drop, brag to make us feel as good as those around us. We turn to booze, drugs, food, gambling, anything to make us feel better and to make the pain go away.

I also learned that when a baby is born, she knows only when she is hungry and if she is warm. If she is uncomfortable she cries and waits for someone to come to her and give her comfort.

When the new baby arrives, she had already recorded in her sub-conscious (computer within) the feelings and sounds while she was in the womb. If those feelings and sounds were serene and pleasant, she has, to the time of birth recorded infant happiness, but thus far has no likes or dislikes, no beliefs, no habits, no self doubts or self esteem. However, from that moment on, her computer records with accuracy every sound, sight, smell, feeling, and emotion. The computer keeps recording and everything in this baby's life, good, bad, or indifferent, truth, lie or bullshit. To her computer, it makes no difference whether or not she believes it, or likes it, or understands it. The computer keeps recording and everything in this baby's life will be effected by what the computer records. As the baby grows, she draws on her computer memory to guide her through her life. If she was shown tenderness, kindness, peace, calm, self respect and warmth, she will grow with those attributes and her personality will shine with an aura of love.

O.K. now lets go back to me, Maggie in the womb. My mother is very tense and nervous because the Monster is yelling and hitting and causing stress. Mother and baby become stressed.   Little Maggie is introduced to her new family in her new stressful environment. She therefore grows up in chronic distress. At the sound of her father's voice, she feels fear, she cries, and as she cries, her father yells even louder. Her heart is working overtime pumping constant adrenaline which is the automatic physical response to fear. As she gets older, living constantly in fear, her heart, blood pressure and her entire body is in a continual state of distress. The only way to change the programming is to replace it with other data. I need to change my world full of fear and stress into one of peace, calm and loving people. I know now that just as some people have been brainwashed into religious cults or Naziism, so I have been brainwashed into fear. I am thinking of it now as being brainwashed then being de-programmed in order to return to the real world that is kind and loving, the world in which I belong.

I can only promise you that I will repeat these affirmations daily, and that I will try to reprogram myself, I will, I promise. If it works, great. If it doesn't, so what.

Love M.   P. S. I haven't had a smoke for three days.

Just to Live -
you have to believe that life will go on
with or without you.
You have to be able to reach out
ask for help, tell someone
that you are hurting and wanting.
You need to have courage
and know that
you can face each challenge
and greet each dawn
with a smile and a prayer.
And you need to have
unshakeable faith and courage
and believe that your time to shine will come
like the faith and courage of a daffodil
that is blooming in the snow.

~CHAPTER NINE~

ALONENESS

"The capacity to be alone thus becomes linked with self discovery and self-realization and with becoming aware of one's deepest needs, feelings and impulses".
- Anthony Storr

The Dark Side of Solitude

In the winter of my solitude
all was cold and barren.
My life was frozen in slow motion
as I woke and worked and slept.
There was no rhyme, no reason,
no purpose to my living, no beauty in my soul.
Then slowly, quietly, discretely
into the darkness of my solitude
came little rays of yellow light, tiny gleams
of newborn joy, small glimpses of envisioned hope
that I could cling to and build on;
as the sun warmed the earth,
there came a deeper hunger
to reach an understanding of love of life
and purpose of living
with full expectation of an early spring.

July 5, 1999

Dear Jenny,

Yes, it has made a difference. Yes I am less and less depressed and most important, yes I found a job. It's not great, minimum wage, crummy hours, but I have a job. Now I have to start working on regaining my self esteem. Just ahead of that is finding a decent place to live. These tiny apartments are only about two hundred square feet. They are always full, because welfare will only pay a couple of hundred a month in shelter, so people have no choice. I have a job, I have a choice.

I never would have dreamed that I would live alone. In all my fifty - two years, I have never lived alone. As children we were surrounded at all times by others in the family. Even more so because most places only had two or three bedrooms among ten of us. After I left home I became a nanny to five children. That was an experience in itself. After I married, I had my babies and one sister and one brother lived with us. If you had asked me if I could live alone I would have answered definitely NO. I would be so afraid. But, something has happened to me. I am alone and I'm fine. In fact I am very fine. I enjoy coming home from work and making supper for only me, eating what I fancy or what I like or whatever. Then, if I don't feel like doing dishes I just leave them for tomorrow. I can watch whatever I want on T.V., or even better, not have it on at all. Nobody tells me where to go, how to get there, what to do, and how to do it. Also, being alone, I am forced to be responsible for my own thoughts and actions, and therefore, must be standing on my own two feet.

- How true, must go, love ya. M.

P. S. My mistake, I can't re-gain my self esteem, because I never had one, I was never allowed to build a self. I must accept the falsities and truths in my life and relearn who I am. The degree of relearning I am capable of will depend on how well I face the truth. If I really want to change my life, I must totally understand that I must accept that my childhood was built on false information and replace the bull shit with the truth. To do that I have to start at the beginning. If friends and family seem to be against me, or seem to be putting me down, I must realize the fact that many people cannot face their own weaknesses and therefore feel that they must push others down in order to get up. Because of this, I am being quiet about the changes in my life. Let them all wait and see for themselves. Many will not even know that these changes are taking place, but then most don't know the long, hard road that I am on.

If I fail this time, I can try again and again until I find that certain peace that I know I have been searching for all my life. I want that peace so badly that I am determined to find it.

If I expect to win I will win, if I expect to loose, I will loose. Self love is built through deserving and therefore expecting the best in life and then going out and getting it. I want to be able to live and work and sleep with some amount of joy instead of constant fear.

~ CHAPTER TEN~

TAKING OWNERSHIP

"What is yours is yours, and what is mine, is mine."

My Friend

My heart reaches out to you
because I see you hurting
and I want you to know
that in time you will heal
and when you come to understand
that the past is behind you, where it belongs,
I want you to tie up all
of your hate, guilt, anger and pain
into one small bundle
and give it to me.
I will put it in my pocket
and keep it there for you
until the day that you want it back
to use again as your burden in life, or
I will burn it for you and
scatter the ashes out to sea.
You will no longer own it,
and therefore my friend,
* you will be free.*

3.   Take ownership and responsibility of and for everything that has happened to you and every emotion you have felt since your age of rebellion (usually around the age of sixteen). Before that age you were a child and had no control over you life, surroundings and, lets face it, you couldn't possibly have chosen the life you had, your parents, where you lived, or how you lived. . Again, no yea but I was raped, I was abused, I was forced to take care of my sick grandmother, no giving yourself excuses. For whatever reason you have attracted people and circumstances to you that you felt you desired. The payoff, or excuse for this may have been financial security, a home, your children, your job. No matter what happened to you as a child, you are responsible for walking around with a sign on your back that reads "kick me". When you have taken all the kicking you can stand, loose the sign, get rid of it!

If you feel trapped by your surroundings, remember, you are where you are not because of others, but because you are exactly where you want to be. If that were not true, you wouldn't be there. If you choose to stay there, you are choosing not to pay the price for change. That price is high, it takes commitment and hard work. If you are too lazy, or too much into the comfort of your own little corner of the world, then for heaven sake, stop complaining about it. Do you think everyone in your world enjoys hearing your constant jabber about how unhappy you are when you won't lift a finger to help yourself? Do you think they all feel sorry for you as you wallow in your own self pity? In a word, "NO".

September 6, 1999

Dear Jenny,

Here goes with number three. This one is tough because I feel I never caused any of the grief in my life. I came into adulthood preprogrammed with all the fear, insecurity, immaturity, need, and whatever other built in crap I have had to deal with. I felt life was unfair, and I felt life was one long continual struggle against fear. The worst fear of course is the fear of fear itself. That really sucks, because I have spent so many years being afraid of something that does not yet exist - the future the next few minutes, the next hour, day, month, year. I have always felt there is no such thing as love it exists only in books, movies and our imagination, that no-one ever loved me, people in my life just wanted to use me because I was there to be used.

If we are deprived of certain physical nutrients, then we develop certain physical deficiencies. Lack of sufficient quantities of any of the vitamins in the diet results in a vitamin deficiency diseases. With replacement of the nutrients, our bodies can (generally speaking) heal themselves.

If we are deprived of certain psychological and emotional nutrients, such as love, nurturing and acceptance, we do not learn how to love and accept ourselves and we develop certain psychological and emotional illnesses. Webster defines deficient - "wanting some element or characteristic necessary to completeness" . When a child is deprived of elements necessary to completeness, the brain automatically produces defense mechanisms necessary for survival.

One of these defense mechanisms is the imagination. If I can detach from my past, and live in my fantasies, then the hurt goes away. The rest of the world keeps turning without me. The more I stay in my imagination, the less I contribute to my job, my family and the rest of the world around me. I can't remember what I did this morning, or what I did five minutes ago, and I can't focus on the real world when I am living in a fantasy world. Living in fear of everything, everywhere I go, everyone I see, every time the phone rings, I am stressed because I am so afraid that I won't say or do the right thing, that people will think me a fool or, more than that, I will prove the Monster right that I am a useless thing, not a person, but a thing. I am prepared at all times to say "I'm sorry" because I don't know what the world or the people in it expect of me.

I never understood that all the bad things in my life, although they were a result of my childhood, were caused by me. I am convinced now that I can make my life better. I also realize that the world around me can only be changed to the extent that I can recognize and change the beliefs that were so deeply ingrained in my sub- conscious as a child. In other words, if I am happy right at this moment, I am in a "happiness" state of mind; conversely, if I am miserable right now, I am in a "misery" state of mind. No one can change that, only me, and only if I have come to the realization that so much of what I learned to believe as a child is wrong. If I let something upset me and let myself go easily from happiness to misery, why can't I do the reverse? I can choose happiness or misery, and therefore I have taken responsibility for my own state of mind. No person, thing or force can make me think something I don't want to think, that fact is a realization in itself! If I decide to choose happiness, I decide to choose unconditional happiness. That in itself is positive motivation.

I guess taking responsibility for my own life also means taking responsibility for my own dreams. I mean dreams of the night time kind . I have never imagined that I would ever figure this one out.

For a number of years, I had a re-occurring dream. I dreamed, time after time, that I was driving a car and my eyes close shut and I can't open them. My eyes in the dream are literally stuck shut, but the car keeps moving. I panic because I have no control over what might happen then, of course, I wake up. Finally, just a few months ago, I realized what the dream meant.

Before I could do that, I had to understand what dreams are. Dreams play a vital part in the workings of our main computer. The computer keeps sorting, constantly, all of the information we take in every moment of every day. The information is sorted into "files" along with other like information. If the computer can't make sense of a certain piece of information, or it can't find a file to put a certain thought into, it gets filed in the dream file to be re-hashed at night and made sense of. If it continues not to make sense, it becomes the re-occurring dream. When finally the person realizes what the dream means, the re-occurring dreams stop.

Back to the dream. I am driving a car. I have always had a deep fear of driving, again a flash-back to "you will never drive, you stupid woman" and "turn here, HERE, you clueless bitch" etc. etc.. The other huge fear

61

is that of having to be in control of a vehicle means I have to be in complete control. Our conditioning was to not think for ourselves, but while driving a car we have to think and not only for ourselves, but for others. In the dream, if I crash, it can't be my fault because I can't open my eyes.

In real life, I couldn't be blamed for anything as long as I was doing as I was told. As long as I depended on someone else to tell me what to do, then, I could just blindly go through life and my "accidents" would be someone else's fault.

I really do not want to live where I am living, work in a minimum wage job, I don't want to suffer any more over my past, my father, my husbands, the poverty, the grief, the horror. I want to be a human being, warm, loving and caring; and, I am not too lazy or too comfy. I will work very hard on caring about myself and choosing the good things in life. It is very difficult to learn to care for myself and not to stop thinking I got what I deserve.

It is only now that I realize my part in contributing to the perpetuation of abuse. I blamed my abusers, loved them, hated them and really believed that it was my mission to help them. Never once in all my years of being a battered wife did I even entertain the thought that I was causing any part of what was happening to me. I wasn't aware that I was causing it, but because of my inability to face life, my ingrained fear that whatever I did would be wrong, I believed that I deserved to be punished. By failing to understand this, I was refusing to accept responsibility for being human. I could pout, sulk, cry, be resentful, complain, become ill, suffer from chronic depression and I couldn't see that I was causing it all. Just as my husband needed me as a kicking post on which to vent his anger and force his control, I used and needed my husband as a receptacle for all my emotional garbage and my inability to live and function in the real world. - Don't even think about it, I'm just not ready to tackle number four - yet. Love Maggie.

November 12, 1999

Dear Jenny,

Two years have past since I left Mark and I am still trying to treat myself with respect and caring. It has taken a long time just to realize that there is no magical healing or fast fix for the scars I carry. I am trying to recognize successes I have and praise myself. I now look straight into my own blue eyes in the mirror and say: "Maggie, you are good, girl. You are smart, good looking (ha ha) and you can and will make it. For so many years, I would fix up my house, in case the neighbors came by. I would bake and cook for people, give and or lend money, sew clothes, cut hair, let people drive my car and return it without gas. It was almost as if I were walking around looking for new things to complain about. I was really "Miss Good to Mankind" in hopes of praise, in hopes that people would tell others what a wonderful, giving person I am without knowing that I am searching endlessly for attention. I would spread myself so thin doing for others and I know now that no-one ever cared, no-one gave a shit about me. No one will think of me as St. Maggie. No, they will think of me as that silly - what's her name who was married to Mark and used to cut hair and sew clothes - for free.

One thing that still brings instant tears to me is any show of emotion or love between a Daddy and his little girl. Whether in reality or on T.V. it still chokes me up. If I could have wished for only one thing as a child, I would wish for a real Daddy who loved me instead of hating me. As a child, little did I know that I would spend most of my life searching for that love. When I see so much beautiful warmth and love between my son and his daughter, it makes me feel that they are blessed, that I am blessed, it warms my heart.

The Monster showed us no affection at all. In fact if any of us kids hugged or kissed one of our siblings, he would yell "Get away from her, you'll make her soft". In other words, he wanted us to be hard, tough, unloving and cold hearted. It didn't make us hard, but we didn't know how to show affection either because we would associate affection with fear, with being reprimanded. I am really starting to feel better, I feel like I am getting a grip. Sometimes I fall into the pit again, but I have made some footholds and I left a rope so that when I feel myself falling,   I can get back up again,   and   when I   start   to feel   the   pain   of remembering, I can say to myself, "Come on, you can do it, it was all a nightmare and you are learning to accept that. "

Love Maggie.

P. S. This next part might do me in.

~CHAPTER ELEVEN~

BARFING

"To regret one's own experiences and not be able to face them, is to arrest one's own development. To deny one's own experiences is to put a lie into the lips of one's own life. It is no less than a denial of the soul".
- Oscar Wilde

Fear -
in this less than perfect world,
I am afraid of love
and life, and loud noises.
I am afraid to cry,
to challenge, to admit
to feeling alone
and always wanting
to change my life.
And so life passes me by,
lost in my dreams,
a comfort zone where I am
always looking for safety,
a crutch, someone
or something to lean on,
needing to change,
to start a journey, but
afraid of what I might become,
and even worse,
afraid to travel alone.

4. You have to be willing to go through the pain to get to the other side. We have all heard the phrase "I can't stomach it", well then barf it.. You have to. You have to barf it all up, sort through it, flush it and go on with your life by being good to yourself.

This includes giving up booze, drugs, or what ever you may have or still are using for easing the pain of the soul. If you hate your job, apartment, husband or whatever or whoever you feel you are stuck with, get rid of it. Oh yes, you can, - give yourself full permission. Stop worrying about how you will live, how you will manage. You will live and you will manage. There are people, groups, churches, agencies, and governments out there to help you. Go to them and ASK for help. No-one is going to seek you out and offer help, you have to ask. If you find this hard, have an understanding friend ask for you.

If you find that others seem to be against you, realize the fact that many people cannot face their own weaknesses and therefore feel that they must hurt others in order to feel good themselves. Because of this, be quiet about the changes in your life. This way if you fail, simply try again. Heaven knows you have felt failure in your life, you can and will succeed. You will keep trying until one day you can say to yourself "Hey, I did it, I am a winner". Self love is built through knowing that you can and will win.

January 5, 2000

Dear Jennifer,

O.K., it's a brand new century and I think I am ready to start barfing up all the nasty stuff. But, I want you to know that the truth can only be my truth or the truth as I see it. My life therefore, can only be as I have perceived it - true or untrue, real or false.

I grew up hating and fearing my father so much that fear overcame my life and I knew no other way of life other than living in fear.

I hated him for fathering so many children knowing he could not provide for them. I hated him for fathering them out of sheer lust and not love. I hated my father for calling me a slut and a whore, for the horrible sickening smell of his breath and even worse the smell of his hands. I hated him for the knowing ache in our stomachs when we went to bed hungry, and for the filth, the lack of pillows and blankets on those beds. I hate him for the smell of the piss bucket on a hot day and the smell of him and his clothes when he hadn't bathed for who knows how long. I hate him for making us go to school without books or boots, or decent, clean clothing. I hate him for his huge bellowing, sharp, cutting voice that would rivet fear so indescribably into our very soul. I hate him for all the things he would not allow: laughter, tears, anger, joy, pain, happiness, sadness, excitement, boredom and worst of all, we were not allowed to think. The only emotion we were allowed to show was fear which gave him the control he needed.

Even to this day where others would feel anger, I feel

fear. I hated him for dying with out realizing or having any understanding of what he had done to us.   I was not, at the age of eighteen, ready to have a child. After I left, or was told to leave my father's house, I clung to my boyfriend, Denny with all my might, even though I was still very much in love with "my own true love", that remained my secret.   Denny found me a place to live with a nice family and found me a job. I was so fearful of everything that he became everything to me. It was the policy of most companies back then that any woman who became pregnant had to quit work after the third month. I lied for an extra month, but once I started showing, I had to quit.

I also had to see a doctor, if I didn't, there would be no doctor responsible to attend the birth and I didn't want that. The doctor was quite kind. He told me that he would have to examine me and that he realized how afraid I was. He had no idea. He told me to take a deep breath and relax. The examination wasn't painful but his question was - he asked "Were you raped when you were quite young, or have you been injured in this area?" My heart began to pound and I felt as if I couldn't breathe - I started to cry.

"It's O.K., Margaret, deep breaths, you don't have to tell me. You have a lot of scar tissue in the vagina and the entrance to the uterus. When you give birth, you will need all of those muscles to push the baby out. It may be very difficult for you. Other than that, my dear, all is well. I would suspect you are in your sixteenth week."

I couldn't wait to get out of there, I felt faint, my face was flushed and sweat was running down my sides and tears down my cheeks.

Denny found me a job as a nanny and housekeeper for a family with five kids in return for room and board. The work was really demanding, so were the kids. I stayed there until a week before my baby was due. Then Denny found us an apartment. It had no running water but otherwise O.K. and cheap in back of an Insurance Agents. There had been no heat on all winter so when the stove was lit, the plaster ceiling in the living room crashed down all over our few belongings.

My pregnancy went three weeks overdue (at least to my calculations, and what did I know?). I woke around 6:am in labor. The hospital was twenty miles away and we had no car (being young, we hadn't thought of that). Denny borrowed the Insurance Agent's car and dropped me off at the hospital. I didn't see him again for over two weeks. After all, it was in the middle of hockey play-offs. I was scared and alone. There was no one there to tell me what to do, or what would happen to me. As the pains became harder and closer I began to panic. I had only seen a doctor once during the pregnancy and I had no idea what was happening to me. I didn't even know exactly how the baby would get out. The pain became unbearable I cried out for my mother, I screamed "please Mom, please come and help me." A mask was held firmly over my face and I was told to breath, so I did. I caught a glimpse in the overhead mirror of the crown of Christopher's head. After that they gave me a needle and I woke several hours later. My legs were still in stirrups and my arms were in leather straps at the wrists. A nurse came in and asked me if I was sure I was eighteen and started pushing the bed down the hall. I was wheeled into a room that had three other mothers. The nurse told me Christopher had been a forceps delivery and I was badly ripped so my legs had to stay "up" so that the air could get to me down there. She let my arms loose and hooked up a lamp pointed at the ripped parts and left. It was a couple of hours before they brought Chris in. I tried to nurse him, but in this position of my bottom being higher than my head it was hard. After about twenty minutes, they took Chris away again. I started to cry. I had no tissues. Tomorrow should be better.

It wasn't. The nurses came and went with the baby every four hours. Chris had latched on pretty good, but the milk was all collecting in my upper chest as my legs were still up in the air. Feeding him became very painful. Also every four hours, the nurse would come in and push a tube up me and drain out the urine. I was allowed to eat, if someone could help me, no-one came. I had a husband, a mother and father, seven brothers and sisters and no-one came. I cried a lot that night.

They had left the IV in "just in case" they had to sew me up again. Then next morning, the girl in the next bed peeked around the curtain and asked if she could come over and eat breakfast with me. I of course was happy, she did help me. She also gave me tips on nursing. The day nurse told me I was a real mess down there and the doctor would be in to see me.

In mid-morning two nurses came in and wheeled me back into the delivery room. The doctor arrived and told me that I would have to be re-stitched as there was some infection and some of the stitches had come out. They froze my lower parts and sewed me together again.

I was in the hospital for fifteen days. Denny never came to see me. I felt as if I had been abandoned. There was a phone at the nurse's station, but it was long distance to everywhere, we had to pay up front to use it, I had no money and, I couldn't get out of bed to walk down there. My bottom end healed very slowly and the hardest part was still coming when they finally led me into the cubicle and told me to pee, oh God, the pain.

On the fifteenth morning, the nurse again led me into the cubicle and told me I could go home after the doctor "took a look" that afternoon.   Just as I hadn't planned on getting to the hospital, I had no idea of how I would get back home. Of course, all the other moms went home after two or three days, so I didn't have the chance to get to really get to know any of them. The doctor came in and for the umpteenth time looked at my "mess down there". When I started crying, he asked me what was wrong and I told him I had no way home. He said he knew of another patient from my town going home that day and he would ask for a ride for me. I dressed Christopher up in the little outfit that I had knitted, he was so tiny, so innocent. I packed the rest of my stuff and waited.

By four o'clock I was standing on the sidewalk in front of the Insurance Agent's with my baby, my suite case and my tears.

The door was open - all the mess from the ceiling falling in was still there and it was cold. I checked the stove, no oil,   I didn't know what to do. Chris started crying. I picked him up and cried again for my Mom, but I knew she couldn't come and I knew it was me and

Christopher against the world. I walked to the gas station. I still had no money and I felt so weak that my knees were shaking.   I asked, no, actually, I pleaded for some stove oil and for someone to put it in for me. Old Fred laughed and said "I suppose you want someone to light the friggin thing for ya too" - "Oh yes - please".

The apartment slowly warmed up and April turned to May, and May to June. My "down there" healed up and the baby grew fat and happy - at least until he was sixteen. But that's another story.

I loved Chris with the fierceness of a mother tiger. My whole world revolved around him I guess you could say I spoiled him but I loved him so much. I worked at the local doctor's office, making appointments and cleaning etc. - Chris went along with me which was good as I could continue nursing him, so - free milk and, of course, I didn't have to pay a baby sitter. I was earning one dollar an hour, which in those days wasn't bad.

The rest of my family had again moved to a nearby town. They were not allowed contact with me. When Chris was twenty months old, at Christmas, I thought I would try a visit. I so much wanted my Mom to see the baby, her first grandchild. I took presents for all the kids and boldly knocked on the front door. There was silence from within, but I could see the curtains moving. I knocked again and waited. The door opened a tiny crack and my brother said, "You are not allowed to be here, you know that Maggie, he won't let you in". The door closed. I left the presents on the front porch and went home heartsick without understanding how a mother could reject her own child.. I didn't try again.

Denny was a good father, when he was home.

He was very involved with his job and quite often worked late, then went for a few beers, leaving me at home with Chris most of the time. Denny also loves hockey and became the coach of the local men's team which took him away even more.

When Chris was three, one of my brothers age eighteen and one sister age sixteen had left my father's house and had come to live with me. They were both so thin, so haggard looking as if they couldn't cope anymore. Of course they had very little in clothes and belongings. It reminded me of the day I left home, all of it filled one paper grocery bag. My brother didn't want to trouble me, but he told me about the horrors at home. At this time the family was living on a farm about twenty miles from me and about forty miles from the city. The Monster drove them each day into the city to work. After work, winter or summer, it didn't matter, Mom and at least two of the teenaged kids would sit in the car and wait outside a bar for hours while the Monster got drunk. Then he would stagger out and drive home. It was really a miracle that they weren't all killed. No one (except for the Monster) was allowed to drive, ever. Mary had tried, several times, but he would shout at her, grab the wheel, and make her cry. She never did learn to drive, neither did Harold.

Just before he left the farm to come and live with me, the kids had found five little kittens had been born in the barn. They were so fluffy, so sweet, scampering around and playing. When the Monster found out not only that there were kittens, but that the kids had been feeding them, he got the gun and demanded that Harold dig a hole. Harold was horrified, the Monster made him finish digging the hole, go and fetch the kittens from the barn, put them into the hole and shoot them one by one.

Both Harold and my sister Becky stayed with me for a couple of years. They both found jobs and we all tried to give each other emotional support but just talking about home and the Monster would bring tears and of course we had never been allowed to cry. Other than to give them a home, I wasn't really equipped to help them. My sister was really depressed, but I was battling my own depression and couldn't be much help to her. My brother was so thin and pale and although sometimes he would talk about the horrors of "home", you could see the pain in his eyes. Denny was really very good to them and helped them in any way he could, but Denny had no understanding of harshness of our childhood.

When Chris was four, Keith was born. I was in labor for what seemed forever - three days, he was crossways in the womb. Finally, the doctor went in and turned him head down the cord was around his neck. Again a forceps birth, but in a hurry. I was awake this time. Everything seemed O.K. for a while until one night after we had been home a week, he stopped breathing and turned blue. We drove the thirty miles with him to the Children's Hospital, they said he had some bleeding under the skull. Yes he did live and yes he was damaged and yes I could still scream over why they did not give me a C section. Of course that was the 1960's and we lived in a small town. Doctors were still being paid with a sack of potatoes and a couple of chickens, but somehow, the doctor had to be paid, so poor people simply didn't go to the doctor unless it was

an emergency. Today it would have been an emergency.
  As a result of his birth, Keith was deaf and that fact alone took a great deal away from his childhood. It also left him venerable for kids at school bullies to push around. I protected him sometimes too much. He found life difficult and soon learned the survival tactic of living in the imagination, sometimes too much.   I didn't know how to guide him into reality because I was living in my own imagination.

  I am starting now to understand so much more about life, it is amazing. Every day I feel that my life has more worthwhile. I used to be my own worst enemy, I am now becoming my own best friend.

Love Maggie

Rain

Warm rain droplets,
 zigging here zagging there,
down the window pane blurring my world.
Trees, houses, streets, all out of focus
just as my life had become out of focus.

Sunshine warming the glass.
Drying the rivulets of rain
leaving only small streaks
to remind me of when my life
was one big blur.

CHAPTER TWELVE

CHRISTOPHER'S LAMENT

Sometimes, in the blackness of the night
he would hear his father's voice.
Calling, caressing filling his mind
with sad sweet memories
of feelings that were real to him;
laughing, running, feeling the peace.
As if a son had been the only purpose
of his father's life.
Who were they? His father and his mother -
his flesh, his blood, his soul.
Who were they to let him fall into a hell
where living causes pain?
All is unfair, for as a child he is not a person
but a possession of one or the other
being told how he should feel.
Who were they to take his everything
and without a tear divide it equally between
them tearing him apart.
He was too big now to cry
or mask his anger with a smile.
And so he showed his anger in hatred,
hatred of the people who had broken up his world
until the pieces had been lost
and he was left to sink into the solitude
in the depths of his mind where sometimes
in the blackness of the night
he would hear his father's voice.

June 4, 2000

Dear Jenny,

As with so many couples who marry in their teens, we grew apart instead of together. After almost ten years, we had become emotionally detached and drifted apart to the point of no return. We separated. I only know how to love in my imagination. In all the remaining years of boys growing up, Denny never once sent a check, a Christmas gift or even a card. No birthdays came without Christopher looking for a card from his father, but it never happened. Keith was only four when we split up and as he was born deaf, he never really realized what was going on and has no memory of his real father. I will never in my life forgive Denny for literally abandoning his own children. Especially Chris who has been very, very hurt and the scars still show. I wrote that poem for him when he was about ten. I was ashamed that I let it happen to him, but like most things in my life, I didn't know how to make the hurt go away.

In the meantime, I had met Gary. By the time we moved out west, Gary and I and the two boys had made a separate family and I no longer had to think about Denny. He had chosen to stay out of our lives and I accepted that. (This next barf up will be hard for me to recount.)

Anyway, we moved out west and life had been pretty good to us. Gary was a well paid professional who would never be out of a job and we would never have to do without. He was raised in a frugal family so he wasn't frivolous either. The boys did hockey, ball, cubs, took music etc. . He took us camping, fishing and did all the "guy" things with the boys; they called him "Dad".

When Chris was sixteen, Gary applied for and got a better job in another western city. We put the house up for sale and of course, like all kids, the boys weren't too happy about it. Keith never did say too much about what was on his mind, but Chris sure did. The night before we were to hit the road, we took a motel room and Chris was to stay with friends. Next morning we went back to the house to make sure every-thing was O.K. - there was Chris and two of his friends still drunk from the night before.

The memory that day haunted me for many years, the picture of Chris and friends walking down the road with what was left a case of beer. I felt tremendous guilt, first Chris had been abandoned by his father and now his mother was leaving him behind. He refused to go with us so we left him there. What else could we do.

Jenny, I can't do any more of this right now - it HURTS. Love Maggie.

August 5, 2000

Dear Jen,

I will try to describe what I am going through with this barfing exercise.

Imagine a large cupboard and every time you encounter something nasty in your life, you open the cupboard and throw it in so you don't have to face it. As time goes by, you throw more and more nasties in the cupboard. When the door is shut, you don't have to face the contents, you don't have to think about it, out of sight, out of mind. The only time they cause you pain is when you open the door to throw more in. The cupboard becomes full and every time you open the door, the nasties spill out all over and you can't avoid them any more.

What I am trying to do now, is open the cupboard and sort out everything that has piled up in there. I am trying to examine the rotten stuff from my past, throw away the garbage and make neat piles out of the rest. Now, I can emotionally cope with opening in the door as most of what is in there is at least been tidied up and is understandable.

I have done a lot of research on abuse and I don't want to sound clinical, but I can now understand a lot of the info as it fits into my life. The following is a description of my marriage to Mark. I guess it is barfing it up but more than that it is understanding the relationship. Mark, pitiful in his search and endless need for power, looked for a mate who would feed his needs. He would not marry a strong, self assured "together person", and his big attraction to me was the fact that I was a woman whose self esteem had been crippled in childhood. He fed his need for power by demanding my constant attention. I would be expected to neglect myself to please him, always ready to satisfy his constant commands. His appetite for attention and sex was never satisfied, so he demanded more and more. Because his demands and need for power were constant and I was only human, he blamed me for everything, even the failure of his first marriage. He did this by using humiliation, criticism, sarcasm, threats and other verbal assaults in an attempt to put me down to give himself power. His behavior became totally unpredictable and his moods would swing from pleasant and loving to harsh and hateful. I could never predict what the next moment would bring. This made me feel venerable and so, so needy. I sunk further and further into the typical roll of co-dependent.

In his need to be in control of me, he would coerce me into doing exactly what he wanted by using scare tactics forever playing on my compassion, fear and guilt. If these tactics were not working, he would threaten to leave me, kill me, kill the children, or kill himself.

He would find fault in and criticizes everything I did (unless that thing was in answer to his command). My cooking, my house cleaning, my roll as step-mother to his children, everything. He would criticize me to family and friends, make fun of me, blowing my mistakes out of proportion and blaming me for his own wrong doings, while belittling and discounting my achievements. When he was accused of molesting an eleven year old, Shelley, from two doors down the street, of course he blamed it on the fact that he was drunk and that I wasn't giving him enough sex so it was my fault. I was the one to face her parents and feeling so hugely guilty, I apologized over and over again. It took about five years before I realized that I had become my mother and married my father. I started to doubt my own sanity. A lifetime of abuse had altered and disfigured my ego and esteem so much that I became a prisoner of my own fears. Unable to understand my feelings realistically, I became numb and I clung to Mark, even though I knew better, I couldn't face any other way of life. I lived in a make believe world and hated myself and Mark and our life together. I started to believe that I deserve the criticism, accusations, insults and assaults, believing that I was unworthy of love. I felt trapped and in my own mind, I was trapped , so afraid of life that just the thought of being alone would bring on a panic attack. I had become my own worst enemy but of course I couldn't see that then.

Both of my boys were grown at this point but Mark had two little girls living in his house of horrors. I tried my best to explain things to them, I don't know how much of it was understood. I kept hoping they wouldn't grow up and be like me.

I realize now that Mark felt powerless in his life. He grew up in a rural uneducated family and was abused himself as a child. His mother would make him go out and cut a willow branch so that she could beat him with it. She used to tell him that he was bad even when he thought he was good. As he grew older, his feelings of powerlessness increased. He didn't do well at school, and couldn't get along with the teachers. (They have power). As he grew to be a man, the pain also grew. When the pain became too much to bear, relief came in the form of a "power packed temper tantrum".

He started drinking in his teens. As with many abusers, he would blame alcohol for his "blow ups" . There is much less guilt involved when he doesn't remember what he said or did because he was drunk. In this way, he could avoid any self responsibility for his words and actions. I could see it building in him, the need for a blow-up. Just like with my father, the blow-ups, or trips off the deep end would be were a high for him. As his power reserves became depleted, his need or a high became greater and greater. I knew that my life would be a constant struggle as long as I stayed with Mark, but that was not what I wanted in my life. I had grown up in that same fear, it was indescribably horrible.

As time went by, I started suffering from stress related illnesses. Migraine, panic, stomach ulcers, bowel disorders, agoraphobia and my old friend depression, and alcohol abuse. The more severe my illnesses became, the more reliant I was. I sent him conflicting messages. I hated him, but I couldn't survive without him.

When we first fell in love, sex to me was beautiful, filled with emotion and love. It seemed that Mark needed me with such passion that I felt he must love me. Over time sex it became a duty in a world blurred by beer, and I would avoid it. If he threatened violence then I would give in. I began to feel emotionally detached from him and had no sexual desire for him any more. I have since learned that a man needs sex in order to fulfil his emotional needs and desires; a woman first needs to fulfil her emotional needs in order to desire sex. My emotional needs were huge, but fulfillment was not to be.

Jenny, my oldest and best friend, I am not great at showing appreciation, or thanking people, but you have been there for me through all of this. I am so, so grateful that you have listened to me for so long and with so much patience. What ever would I have done if I hadn't had a friend.

Love, Maggie

~CHAPTER THIRTEEN~

BELIEFS

"As you are taught as a child, so you will believe that to be true. However, the past exists only in memory. Consequences of the beliefs of childhood have power over you only as you can release them, let go and move freely into the future."

5. Make a list of all the beliefs that you have carried since childhood and how they have changed to what they are today. Authoritarian parenting is parenting that forces children to learn by submission, no reward, only punishment, sometimes brutal punishment. Therefor the child learns that the only way to gain approval is by total compliance. This also encourages the child not to think for him or herself, only to do as he/she is told. In your effort to change your world, you must change most of your basic beliefs as your healing progresses, you may want to add more beliefs to your list.

October 10, 2000

Dear Jennifer,

Here is a list of beliefs I learned as a child that were untrue or false and I have carried through my life:

- Believing that my past is responsible for my future. While it is true that my past has made me what and who I am today, I did not believe that I could change the future, but I can make it what I want it to be.

   - Believing that "I made my bed and therefore must lie in it". When I married, I expected to be mistreated. I believed that I was not worthy of respect or kindness and that no matter what, I had to live that way.

   - Mistrusting myself and all my God given intuition. Because I learned as a child to only receive instruction from someone other than myself, I believed that I was incapable of sensible thought, and that I was the last person on earth capable of guiding myself. Any thoughts or feelings of my own were only fantasies, day dreams, not correct, not real.

   - Thinking that everything and every person in life is good or bad, right or wrong, black or white. I was taught that there was no in between, no grey area, so that everything and everyone had to be one extreme or the other. It was this belief that caused me to express everything in extremes. I couldn't simply be not feeling well, I had to have the worst cold, headache or disease known to mankind. Or I had to be the best, a perfectionist, the best cook, the best mother, the best person alive.

   - Lying, or stretching the truth in order to gain esteem, credibility, praise and recognition. Because all of those qualities are essential to the healthy growth of self, and I was given or shown none of the above as a child, as an adult, I would lie or exaggerate my childhood, my education, knowledge, position in life or almost anything that would add sensation to my story and make people believe that I was O.K. when I actually believed that I was not O.K..

- Feeling through a sense of loyalty that I had to defend myself, my abusive husband, my children, parents and family. I was taught and therefore believed that family loyalty and patronage should be automatic and unquestioned. I therefore would defend my family whether I felt or believed them to be right or wrong.

- Prejudging myself and others using the strict unquestionable rule of my childhood. I had been taught and therefore believed that people should be judged in accordance with their ethnic background, color, religion, politics, education and status in life.

- Believing that I could not change, but others could. I could not be wrong because, after all, I was just a little sheep following others, never making my own decisions, so that anything that happened in my life was the fault of someone else. I believed that I was as I had been taught, so firmly planted in my beliefs, and that I could not change.

- Not knowing or understanding myself and my motivations and therefore having no understanding of others and their motivations. The basic motivation of my childhood was fear. I was taught to be afraid of everything and every situation. I worked, played, lived, breathed and slept in fear of what would happen if I weren't afraid. Therefore, I had no understanding of those who worked, played, lived, breathed and slept just for the sheer joy of it.

- Believing that I was unworthy of love and respect and yet constantly searching and striving for any kind of recognition. I would constantly try to impress others, do and care for others trying to gain love and respect for myself.

- Believing that I was trapped, that I was destined to live in bondage for the rest of my life, not realizing that fear alone was my master.

- Believing that I was dependent on others for all of my needs and that I could not be self reliant. I did not realize that I couldn't fall unless I was leaning on someone. I had a great need to be told what to do, expecting to be punished if I didn't do as I was told.

- Believing that the needs of others must come before my own and that being kind to myself was being selfish, and self centered,. I believed that I was not a unique, whole person, but somewhat like a robot.

- Depending on the approval of others in order to feel good about myself. I was taught and therefore believed that if I felt good about myself, I was being selfish and vain. I couldn't even buy and item of clothing without first having the approval of another person in order not to feel the guilt.

- Constantly complaining about my life but doing nothing to make it better. Again, fear was ingrained in my thinking, especially the fear of change. Complaining gave me attention that I craved. I became a "yes - but" person. Whenever advice was offered, I would agree, "yes, but I can't do that because- - -" I could never admit that I was afraid because I believed that fear would bring me disrespect and I would be judged as a weak person. And so I went on and on through the years making excuses for myself. My whole life was an excuse - "Yea but I was abused" so I can't face life.

- Not really listening and therefore not understanding what people were saying, but re-analyzing their thoughts, or concentrating on what I was going to say next, or the point I wanted to make. My childhood taught me to filter out or block out what was being said and to concentrate on how I could gain praise or avoid punishment in what would be my reply.

- Believing that I had to accept the pitiful person and pitiful life that had been created for me and that I had no power over my life to change it.

- That emotions were not real, or were not supposed to be real. I was taught that I could only cry if I were bleeding or injured; that my life was predestined to misery and so I had no right to feel joy.

- Believing that my body and my sexual desires were nasty, dirty and wrong. That a female body was for the use and abuse of men.

For myself, change of any kind would produce stress. Too much stress would produce panic. Just the thought of panic produced extreme fear of insanity. I had to hang on very tightly, with so much stress, in order to keep myself sane, I would avoid fear by avoiding the thought of panic by avoiding stress and therefore avoiding change.

One of my first lessons in life was to obey or be punished, I therefore learned fear. I believed that the Monster dominated my life, but it was fear that dominated me and fear that I had to overcome.

They say that if you are afraid of something, that if you can face that fear, you can overcome it. If you are afraid of everything, life itself, then it is a little more complicated. You can face the fear time after time and you can panic time after time, however, the fear remains. It is like soldiers going into a battle, no matter how many times they must go into combat, the fear of dying is always present but they must go over and over again.

What I needed to do was go ahead and feel the fear and then deal with it calmly and quietly and without panic, so that each time I had to repeat facing the fear, I would become more and more confident that I am a strong and serene person and no matter what the fear, I can handle it. - I know I can,

Love Maggie

~CHAPTER FOURTEEN~

GOD HELP ME

"It is one of the most beautiful compensations of this life that no man can sincerely try to help another without helping himself"
- Ralph Waldo Emerson

In the Shadow of Fear

I grew up in the shadow of fear
of darkness and chaos and panic.
I grew up afraid and ashamed of each day
of my past, and my feelings and my hatred.
I grew up believing that I was unworthy
of attention or nurturing or happiness.
I grew up never seeing the sun or
the joyous and glorious colors of love.

But, I did grow up,
it was a painful journey that
took most of my life.

December 3, 2000

Dear Jennifer,

Thank you so much for helping me along this rough road to recovery.

I have come a long way since starting on this hard, hard journey. I know now that a big part of my healing process is in having a good understanding of what has happened in my life and why I have suffered so deeply. I wish I could simply say "I am the daughter of an alcoholic", or "I came from a dysfunctional family," and just accept life. I wish it could have been different, I wish I could have had a "normal", "happy" family. As children, we were forced to feel guilty about having fun, laughing, feeling pleasure or joy were all discouraged. Life was about surviving, not living and enjoying.

I see now that much of my adult life was spent in re-opening the wounds of childhood so that I would hurt and bleed over and over again. When we are unloved as children, we continue to search for that perfect "mother love", the perfect mother and child union. We go from partner to partner looking for the love that we never had. Each new lover promises the "perfect love" we have been searching for but each new love ends in a deeper depression, loneliness and sense of self hate and guilt. I have always thought that I would never find real love, the only real love of my life was kept in my imagination. Now I understand that I always felt I was not worthy of love, that I was a slut and a whore just as my father had called me.

As an adult, with my childhood needs still

unmet, I could not develop any further than basic need of dependancy. I continued to live in extreme stress, being afraid of everything and but still trying to survive and cope with my life. Now I have to get past the grieving and go on with my life. I want so much, as I go through all of this, to go back and get my brothers and sisters and take them on the journey with me, to try to help them. However, I know that if they are to be helped, they can only help themselves. We all have to know and believe that the Monster, whoever the monster may be in our life, is not our father. God is our father and he loves us totally and unconditionally. God is within us, he lives within the soul of each and every one of us. It doesn't matter which building we choose to worship, or whether we worship at all. We don't need to know where he lives . Luke 17:21 "the Kingdom of God is within you."

I would pray time after time for Jesus, God, Mary and any number of saints and angels to help me. Now I realize that I am the only one who can help me and that God does help those who help themselves.

Love, Maggie

P.S. I know this must be hard to digest, I hope you can understand it. - On to the next step. This one will take a long time. I am going to start with person who hurt me the most. I thought if I tackle the hardest first, the rest would be easier. M.

~CHAPTER FIFTEEN~

I FORGIVE

"Forgive us our trespasses as we forgive those who trespass against us"
The Lord's Prayer

6. *Write a letter to each and every person that has hurt you or done you wrong in your life and tell each that you forgive them. Then write a letter to each and every person in your life that you have hurt or you have done wrong to and ask their forgiveness. Keep these letters in a safe place for a minimum of three months, then, when you feel comfortable, take them out and read them. If you don't feel healed enough to rip them up, or burn them, put them back for another length of time.*

Father's Day

On Father's Day, I feel so lost
I want to send my love to him but I can't
for, although I had a father
I never had a Daddy.
I see Daddies out with babies,
Daddies in the park playing with
bouncy little kids screeching with delight.
Daddies giving brides away
and proudly being Grandpas.
My father never did those things
he hurt me, cursed me, shamed me,

leaving me with deep ugly scars.
I hated him and that is why
it is the Daddies on Father's Day
that make me cry - and
I miss the Daddy I never had.

Dear Dad,

This letter will be very hard for me to write. But, you see, it is part of my recovery and if I want to recover, I have to do it. Oh my God, I am apologizing to you.

How I hated you although the word hate isn't really a description. Disgust and loathing are two words that somehow fit better. You had to know, Dad how we hated you, how we would hide from you. Maybe not, maybe you were so wrapped up in your own selfish drunk world that you didn't understand anything about us.

After we grew up I hated you for hundreds of reasons. Things like kicking me out into the world as you did all the kids at the age of sixteen and then rejecting us, disowning us, not even speaking to us again, until you needed money for whatever reason, then of course, your children were expected to be generous. It hurt me to the core that you wouldn't let my mother or my brothers and sisters even speak to me. Did Mom want to? Did she ask you? Did you scream at her and tell her that I was outcast from the family, a disgrace, that I was not worth one second of your thoughts. And what about my children that you refused to see. When I was in the hospital, in labor, crying for my mother, how could you disown and deny your own grandson?

I forgive you for all the wasted years in my life. For all the searching for love that wasn't there, for filling my life with fear and hate instead of hope and love. For robbing me of my childhood, the years that should have been filled with wonderful memories. I forgive you as even at the end of your life when you were full of cancer, you still couldn't talk to us with love and kindness, you still needed to express your power over us and that grip of power still had its effect. I forgive you for the horror when you would turn into the Monster and scream at us and hurt us and even through the crying and pleading of our mother, you would tell us that we were the downfall of your life, that without us, you could have been a great man, as you took another drink. You know, there is an old saying that you can take the booze away from a mean bastard, but you still have a mean bastard.

I forgive you for all the days and there were hundreds that I was ashamed of you, of our home, of our family, and to go to school. For our lack of water, soap, books, clothes, boots, lunches, bras, tampons and everything else that were bare necessities of life. Poverty hurts kids. More important than that, I forgive you for never, ever, once going to school to see out teachers or to see us in a play, or to get an award. I also forgive you for not letting my mother go which would have meant the world to me. I forgive you for the fact that we weren't allowed to take physical education because we didn't have the proper clothes or shoes. I forgive you for the fact that we all have superior intelligence, but none of us received the childhood education to use that intelligence. I forgive you for the fact that we were reported to the health department because we had lice and scurvy and "dirt scabs" from not having a bath for months at a time and bad teeth, but no toothpaste and certainly no dentist.   I forgive you for never allowing us to have friends or birthdays, or parties, or to ever, ever have other children in the house.

I forgive you for making us all into co-dependants by not allowing us to think for ourselves and therefore remain dependent on others to think and act for us, by not giving us the freedom to develop: to think, feel, see, hear, decide for ourselves, instead of constantly being told.   I forgive you for making us obey you blindly therefore giving up our own personalities and deny all emotions which then turned into fear. As our mother lived in constant fear of you, so we mirrored that fear.

By denying us the right to explore our emotions or by denying us the right to laugh or cry or feel anger and pain, you made us regress to our imagination, and when we did, you accused us of being insane.

One incident that I will never forget is one Sunday afternoon, you told me that I couldn't go out to play. Not going out to play was torture, it meant walking on egg shells, not talking, not laughing, not being a child. Getting out of the house when you were there was one of our few pleasures in life. I snuck out, thinking that by supper time you would be drunk and asleep.   Of course you got drunk, but when I got home, you certainly were not asleep. You screamed at me asking me how I dare defy you, asking me who I thought I was to totally disobey you? How could I go out and play with other children not even caring that I had been ordered not to? I started crying and told you that I was a person and had the right to decide. At that, you picked up a chair and threw it at me. It hit the wall. You told me that I was not a person and that I had no rights.   I was so afraid, that I felt I would faint.   My heart was pounding and my breathing had become short puffs. I was ordered out of the room, thank God but even now, I know that being told that I was not a person was one of the scars I carried through my life and over the years that scene would play over and over in my mind. What the hell did you think I was, Dad?, if not a person?

I forgive you for teaching us how to hate. Where other families and other children were learning to love, how to be tolerant of others, we were force fed hate. Anyone who was not a male white Anglo Saxon with fair skin and blue eyes, in your opinion fell short of your expectations of a human being.   You said you hated Hitler and you fought against him in the war, but actually you were a lot like Hitler.   Yes, Dad, you taught us well, we did hate you. Oh, God, how we hated you.

I forgive you for our lack of social graces. Yes you taught us to stay at the table, not speak and keep our eyes on our plates, stand at attention and call you sir, demanding conformity, but you certainly did not teach us how to relate to others, how to be and how to act out there in the real world. How on earth did you expect us to survive out there after living for sixteen years in a fear commune. You would make us watch T.V. programs about war and violence, but you forbid us to watch shows like "I Love Lucy" or "Lassie" or "Disney" because you thought that there was some kind of a conspiracy trying to brain wash young children.

Although many of them would disagree, I forgive

you for and on behalf of my brothers and sisters. I don't think you realized at the time that when you would punish or hurt one of us, you did it to all of us as a family, all of us joined by a common soul. Because our lives were so different from others, it kept us all very close. If one was hurt, we would all hurt. We still all hurt.

As I forgive you for all the horrible pain I suffered, I also want to thank you, because out of horrible pain comes imagination. Imagination is a safety mechanism within our brains which takes over when we cannot stand what is going on around us. Out of imagination comes creativity. Using that creativity, I have constantly searched to discover myself, to find my own identity and to find meaning in life through my paintings, my poetry and my writing. This has given me the capacity to now be alone and to be happy alone. My aloneness is very much part of my self discovery and self realization. The creativity is my medicine and when I am depressed, I can write and paint and bring joy to myself, I feel gifted. Even if this gift is the only gift I ever received from you, it is huge, and again, I thank you.

Now, I want to tell you that I am sorry. I am sorry that in order to validate my life, I had to place blame, so I blamed you for everything that I had become, a self hating, self pitying, chronically depressed , unloving, unloved and most of all, a very fearful person. Using power, and fear tactics, you controlled our lives and as a result, we became slaves which made us prisoners in our own minds. Without any life skills, we could not break the chains that bound us, some of us are still tied and bound to the past.

I am also very sorry that no-one helped you, that no-one could ease your pain. I am sorry that you didn't reach out for help, that you never found God in your life. I remember you telling us that there was no God, that we were not allowed to believe in God because you didn't. It's funny, but you would preach to us about atheism one day and then sing hymns the next.

I remember you singing Lead Kindly Light :

Rev. J. H. Newman, 1833

Lead kindly light amid encircling gloom,
lead thou me on.
This night is dark and I am far from home,
lead thou me on.
Keep thou my feet, I do not ask to see
the distant scene,
One step enough for me.

Did you want to reach out, Dad? Did you want to take steps to be sober, to be a man, a husband, a father instead of a monster.

This is so sad. Just think of how many lives could have been joyous, wonderful if you could have found some peace within yourself. You didn't even feel peace as you were dying. You were screaming in panic. You were so afraid. At that thought I feel such sadness.

While all of the obscenities of our childhood were happening where was our mother? Was she defending us, helping us, showing us love and understanding? No, she, in between bearing children, was feeding children as best she could, worrying constantly that her children

98

might freeze to death because there was no wood cut or oil for the stove or burn to death because her husband in his drunken state has such a fire going that the stove pipes are glowing red. No, she suffered terribly while still clinging to your every word, obeying your every command, not knowing how and too afraid to be anyone else but your slave.

Our mother was totally trapped, or I should say she felt totally trapped, not only by you, but by all of us children. She felt that there was nothing she could do but hope and pray for the best. Her brainwashing had been completed before I was born. She believed in you. What else could she do with eight babies? If she disobeyed you she would have to stand the consequences and the consequences were very hard to take.

If you hated fatherhood so much that you felt you had to sacrifice all life might have held for you, then why did you father us.

You were a rotten dad, we hated you, but you were the only father we had. By forgiving you, I am releasing myself from the grip of your power. I no longer need to make excuses for you or my life. I am free.

Maggie

P.S. I almost wrote " Love, Maggie", just because I am supposed to. Old habits die hard, but I do forgive you.

~CHAPTER SIXTEEN~

DEAR ME

"Sometimes the hardest person to forgive is yourself, but you shouldn't be more critical of yourself than you would be of others."
Anon

Reminders

Emotions emerge from
the very core of our souls;
powerful scenes locked away
in the black cellars of our minds.
They surface and take us by surprise,
thoughts and dreams, long forgotten
fears of childhood days gone by
now vivid reminders of our dark secrets
pushed and forced down the cellar hatch
but the door won't close
and sometimes we have to face
and forgive ourselves
for those desperate emotions that still live
within the darkness of our souls.

February 11, 2001

Dear Jenny,

I had intended to write to several people and forgive them, but now I realize that it was I, not them that I need to forgive. That is much easier to see now that I have taken responsibility for my own life.

Dear Me,

I forgive you, Maggie for the times you have leaned on others and fallen, not realizing that you should have been standing on your own two feet. I forgive you for all the years you hated yourself, that you held yourself back from many opportunities simply because you could not face your fears. I forgive you for all the tears you cried wallowing in self pity. I forgive you for continuing year after year to think you needed a man to fulfil your life. I forgive you for all the years that you were drinking and sometimes drank yourself into a stupor, thinking that booze would be your medicine, make you forget, or make you relax, give you courage and enable you (even through the fog) to go on from day to day as a dependent person, not only dependent on the alcohol, but also on the others in your life.

I forgive you for all your years of smoking and exposing others to dangers of your smoke. I want you to know that I realize that you were addicted to tobacco even as a child. The addiction started when you were still in the womb, your mother and father smoked and when you were a baby, because you were exposed to smoke from the day you were born just as you exposed our own children to your smoke. But, I am proud of you for quitting. I forgive you for blaming others for your own thoughts and actions. By understanding that you were disabled by the demanded conformity that took away your ability to think for yourself, you had to have someone to tell you what to do, and therefore someone to blame.

I forgive you for all of your fears and how you let these fears cripple you. Your fear of confrontation, your fear of love, of anger, fear of hurting people's feelings, or having people dislike you. Fear of dogs and or any number of animals, fear of men in authority or in uniform, fears of being raped, fears of having sex because making love was never about making love it was about being used.

Fear of being hurt, fear of heights and falling, fear of open spaces and closed spaces. Fear of failure which meant that you would not try at all. I know now why you were so afraid and I forgive you.

I forgive you for lying or stretching the truth constantly to cover up your fears and to gain what you thought was respect and recognition. I know most of your lies were petty and didn't effect anyone or hurt anyone, but you were lying nevertheless. Just in order to join in a conversation, you would lie and add stories of your own. Also in order to get attention, your story would always be the best or worst of any other which gave you the attention that you lacked and therefore craved.

And, I forgive you for not loving yourself and for all the years you have wasted in being miserable.
Love, Me

~CHAPTER SEVENTEEN~

FORGIVE ME

"The reason to forgive is for your own sake. For our own health. Beyond that point, needed for healing, if we hold onto our anger, we stop growing and our souls begin to shrivel."
M. Scott Peck

March 14, 2001

Dear Jenny,

Writing letters to and asking forgiveness from all those that I have hurt required a lot of thought. Many people who I think I have hurt in the past may well have overcome those hurts and forgiven me years ago. On the other hand, maybe they didn't, or there may be some that don't even realize that I hurt them, only I think I have, so here goes.

Love, M

Dear Christopher and Keith,

Please believe me, my sons, I have never, ever in my life tried to or intentionally hurt you. I know there must have been times when I did because I was living in a world of my own and suffering from the backlash of my own childhood. Forgive me for the lies I told to protect you from the truth, for loving you too much when love was all I had. Forgive me and believe that I did the very best I could with the limited knowledge and know-how that I had. Like all parents, I guess, there were times in your childhood when I lost it, or when I was so depressed that no-one could reach me. Please believe that from within the ties that bound me to my past, I made the best life for you that I could. Forgive me for the times that I was so lost, so buried in my own grief that I could not hear you crying.

I need for you to forgive me in order to heal the wounds of motherhood. You came from me, you are my flesh and blood, you share my soul.

You have the right to criticize the things I have or haven't, should or shouldn't have done, things I said, couldn't or didn't say.

Forgive me for my sometimes savage devotion. When you were young, I must have been so suffocating, and overprotecting and loving in many ways, and not to love or care at all in many ways. I could not, would not have hurt you the way I was hurt and yet the reality is that through my own suffering, I hurt you. As a child, I was taught so many totally false and totally weird beliefs. I was also taught not to think for myself and not to believe in myself which in my mind meant that I had to have someone to blame for everything in my life.

When your father and I split up, I didn't blame you, Chris, but somehow I thought you felt responsible. I know it broke your heart, you loved your father very much and through the years you were so hurt because you felt abandoned by him. If only he had called you, written to you, anything - but he chose not to and that was his decision.   He also chose not to pay child support. Perhaps I should have hauled him into court, heaven knows he was making good money, but I didn't.

I decided that if he wanted you to learn values (for example " men can father a child and not take any financial responsibility") then I really didn't encourage him to be in your lives. Keith was too young when we separated to remember him. In a way, Keith was blessed in that he didn't feel the abandonment, he didn't hurt over it. Please forgive me, my children for being unable to live with, relate to and love your father.

Also, please forgive me for any choices, beliefs, decisions and judgements made on your behalf that have caused you shame, sadness, pain, disappointment, anger or any other negative feelings. I only meant to love you, Mom.

Oh Mother

Oh, Mother of mine, come hold my hand and
tell me that I am still your little girl.
Tell me that our lives were full of love and fun,
happy days and peaceful nights.
Paint for me a picture of laughing babes,
carefree singing and dancing around you.
Children whose memories would be full
of joy and love and happiness.
Tell me that the hateful times
are not real, they are only dreams,
they never really happened
and I am imagining my sadness
and sorrow, my hate and fear.
Tell me oh mother of mine
for I really need to know, and

*I am desperate
to find peace in my life.*

Dear Mom,

Forgive me please for any time I may have neglected you. For any time I may have made you ashamed of me. For any time I may have been disrespectful toward you, or blamed you for anything that may have happened in my life. I didn't realize that I alone was responsible for the outcome of every day of my life, just as you are responsible for your own happiness. There is no greater love bond than that of mother and child. I came from you and therefor I am and always will be part of you.

I have chosen to no longer be a Victim. I refuse to, over and over again relive the pain and I do not want to use my past as an excuse for today. I am responsible for every day of my life, happy, sad, good, bad, all of it.

Please understand Mom that the memories, emotions and pain of our childhood are my own memories, emotions and pain and I have chosen my own way to recover from them. I know now that you did the best you could with what you had. I also know now that there will be a special place for you in heaven.

God bless you Mom, you tried so hard.

Love Maggie

P.S. To anyone else in my life that may think I have hurt them, please forgive me, and believe me that I had no intention of ever hurting anyone, and the one I hurt the most, of course, was myself.

Secrets

Teardrops that fall quietly onto the pillow
silent crying, screaming from within,
so no one hears the hurting
and no one comes to help and no one cares to ask.
The reason for the teardrops
is her secret kept within
and no one needs to know
and no one understands and no one has the time.
The secret is so dark, so black
it hurts her and pains her
and she just doesn't know
that if she would only tell, people would come and help
and care to ask, and want to know
and understand and take the time
to tell her that despite the dark black secret,
she is loved.

April 4, 2002

Dear Jenny,

I feel like a million tons of weight have been lifted off my back. I have been suffering so much by being unhappy in order to be happy. In our society, suffering is encouraged. We are praised for being "tough as nails". The worst story, the saddest song, the "Oh if you only knew what I went through". The war hero showing scars, how heroic. Of course the truth is "who cares". We may as well all decide to be happy and skip the heroics, because no-one really cares how tough you are.

All the small insignificant and crappy little details of my life, now bared to the world and no one gives a shit. They all have their own war scars to show off and their own dirty little details hiding in the closet.

They say that mourning is a healing process. That is why people attend wakes and funerals. There is no such thing as an enjoyable funeral, but it is something that must be gone through in order to heal from the wounds caused by death and go on with the business of living.

Anyway, even though it was hard to write my letters, it forced me to view the deceased, I have done it and I am glad. I will put them away now and bring them out in three months or so to re-read them. That should be a good cry!

I have been thinking about how far I have come on my road to recovery, I don't like looking back anymore and I am feeling rather proud of myself.

Love Maggie

~ CHAPTER EIGHTEEN~

HERE AND NOW

"Look to this day, in it lies all the realities and verities of existence, the bliss of growth, the splendor of action, the glory of power. For yesterday is but a dream and tomorrow is only a vision. But today, well lived makes every yesterday a dream of happiness and every tomorrow a vision of hope."

Sanskrit proverb

7. Get into and stay in the here and now. Remember, what is, is and what ain't, ain't. The past is gone and neither you, nor anyone else can change that fact. The only thing for sure, as sure as you were born, you will die. It is your choice whether the remainder of your life, no matter how long or short, is a time of peace and contentment or one of despair and anguish. As long as you fill your life with fear, anger, hate and resentment, you can't find love. Love is what you are searching for answers and why you striving to change your life.

November 14, 2002

Dear Jenny,

Staying in the here and now is hard. It means that years of hurting that I have been so used to hashing over and over to " make it hurt" so that I could suffer and be a hero have to be flushed. " Get over it" is a favorite

109

saying of the day, so I have to get over it. I have to turn off any negative anticipation and face problems with a calm and confident attitude. I have to stop being a martyr. Stop worrying unnecessarily. If I have to worry, I must worry positively, constructively. If something needs to be changed, change it for the better.

I also need to understand that all humans are human, we all make mistakes and we should all be allowed to say I'm sorry, learn from the mistake and try again. I have always been afraid of making a mistake. I would suffer from severe guilt and remorse. First though, I would try to pass the buck. If it were someone else's fault, that was fine, I didn't have to stand any consequences.

It always seems that I feel guilty if I don't worry because I feel that I am neglecting something, that I don't care, that I have no conscience . I would put myself into a tail spin and where would it get me? I would worry so much that I would stutter and forget what I wanted to say. Therefor, worrying is a silly habit, born out of fear; fear of losing, fear of failing, fear of abandonment.

I believe that also as a result of my childhood, I am overly sensitive to the emotional tones of voice, (especially hostility) and that I overreact to those overtones. I also grew up believing that I should avoid confrontation of any kind at any cost, because I believed that I would be forced to agree with the aggressor.

I also find that every job I have ever had has been stressful. Actually, I have made it that way by being afraid of those in command. On any job there must be a chain of command in order to ensure that the work will get done in an accurate and timely fashion. The reason is that I have made it stressful is because of fear, I would constantly be worried. I think I will add another affirmation to my list.

- I do not worry. I calmly and quietly tackle problems positively and constructively so that there is no need for worry in my life.

Through the years I have put up "barriers" to keep people away from my heart. I always believed that I was no good, useless and no-one could ever really get close to me because they would see me for what I was, just that. I really need to work on opening up and letting people into my heart. Love Maggie

The Barriers

If I don't let you into my heart,
you cannot break it.
If I don't let you into my place,
you cannot leave me.
If I don't lean on you,
you cannot let me down.
If I don't let you into my mind,
you cannot make me crazy.
If I do not accept your gifts,
you cannot claim me.
If I keep the barriers up,
you can never reach me -
therefore,
why try?

~CHAPTER NINETEEN~

ACCEPTANCE

If Only

The other me that hides in silent despair
and longs to feel the sun, the warmth of living;
longs to be unshackled from cold, heavy chains
made of fear and desperation.
The same chains that have bound me all my life
to the deep dark secrets of my past.

The other me that screams one long hideous cry
help me, look at me, love me.
The other me is not the only me, and
it is I who must let myself be free
to breathe, to live and to love -
if only I could believe in myself.

December 5, 2002

Dear Jenny,

I wish I could say that all is well in my life, but it is taking such a long time to be where I want to be. Sometimes I get discouraged. I don't even think about wanting or finding another man. I still feel as though I don't deserve to be loved and I don't know how to give love. If I did meet another man, I think I would still be too afraid to trust my heart.

I don't mind living alone, in fact I think it is great.

There is no-one here to pass judgement on my life, or the way I live it. On the other hand, there is no-one to give me a word of encouragement, or to give me a hug, or to give me a kick in the ass when I need it, but all in all, the solitude in my life is wonderful. As a child, I always thought I could never go home again, I wouldn't want to, home was a place where you had to be afraid, but not having a home to go to was such a horribly lonely feeling. I always wanted home to be a wonderful warm safe place filled with love. That is the home that I have now made for myself.   I have decorated my rooms in shades of green and filled them with plants making my apartment a really pleasant place to be. I don't care if things doesn't match or the dust bunnies are having babies under the bed, it feels like home. Because I have no money, I have very little furniture. I have no "good stuff" like dishes or pots. I wear uniforms to work and so there is very little need of clothes. My priorities have sure changed.

I used to keep so much clutter around me. Now my surroundings are quite simple, no particular style, just me. I find I no longer need to be a pac rat and save everything. I have for years collected so much "stuff". I think that is because we did without so much as children that having a closet bulging with clothes and cupboards upon cupboards of dishes was important to me. Now it isn't. Now excess baggage is just that, junk. The same as the excess baggage I was keeping in my mind, my computer was full of it. Now I am free of all that stuff. I have survived the horrors of life, now I must let myself enjoy the wonders. The horrors of my life have proved nothing other than the fact that I am a survivor, not a victim.   Sometimes I find that I feel myself going back into the pit.   I was trained all my life to be a mouse, to be afraid of life itself. Sometimes I want to go back to being dependant and want to be taken care of. Those moments are usually times of emotion and deep down I know I only want to go ahead with my life, not back.   This takes some hard work. Sometimes I react to disapproval, failure and loss which gives me an empty feeling and again I feel the need to please. But I now realize that the price of approval is compliance. If forced to comply, I feel hostility toward others which is very depressing.   I now realize that I let everything that happened in my life depend on everything else that had happened in my life.   Every thought, feeling, and decision was dependent on all of the other thoughts, feeling and decisions, most of which were made for me.

Even something simple like accepting a gift, or a compliment. It always embarrassed me when people would show me any kindness. I couldn't just accept and say "thank you", I would get all shucksy and tongue tied. Deep down, I never thought I deserved a gift. When it came time for me to give a gift to someone else, it was a different story. I wanted it to be the most wonderful, beautiful gift ever given.   I was still looking for acceptance, love and appreciation.

These are the times that I must remember that the past is gone. Yesterday will never come again. I can't go back in my life, to live it over or make it better. There is nothing I must do, or be, or have. It is all up to me. All I must do is breathe, eat, sleep and be happy.

To be happy, I need to understand pain, not be afraid of it. I need t learn where it comes from, how and why it hurts me, which emotions bring it on and then turn off and refuse to feel the emotions that cause the pain. It is really that simple, I refuse to feel pain, fear and chaos. I have replaced it with love, serenity and hope.

By learning not to worry, I can tackle each problem with sanity, instead of panic. I can calmly think and reconstruct the problem until quite often it solves itself, or was not a problem in the first place, and I don't even know why I was worried about it.   I see now that many of the problems I have had in the past have not really been problems, but have been blown out of proportion by worry. Worry and guilt go hand in hand. If you are not worrying, you must feel guilty, because we attach worrying to caring. Therefore I would feel that if I am not fretting and stewing over something, I don't care and the world will hate me until I feel such guilt that I must start worrying again.

By staying in the here and now and living and enjoying my life each and every minute of each and every day, I don't have to think of the future, or worry about it, it will come along anyway, it always does.

I suppose you must feel like, O.K., enough is enough already.   Sorry, Jen, I am just so full of all the stuff I have learned it bubbles out of me sometimes. I can't really just stop people on the street and tell them, its just that you have known me all my life, and you understand.

Love, Maggie

~CHAPTER TWENTY~

REMEMBERING

"The mind is its own place, and in itself can make a heaven of hell, and a hell of heaven. If we choose to remember only the sad parts of life, then we will be sad, but if we remember the happy days, then we will savor them and hold them in our hearts."
John Milton

Clouds

Sometimes in clouds
I see the most serene faces
of angels with huge feathered wings.
People who have left this life
and ventured forth
into the beautiful unknown
that we call heaven.
In clouds I see their smiles,
their graceful easy movements
dancing, frolicking across the blue
unburdened by worry or care
sublimely happy just to be.

But sometimes in the clouds,
I see the faces of monsters
that have hurt me and tortured me
and have left my life, my spirit, my soul
in a storm filled sky of despair.

December 29, 2002

Dear Jenny,

Now, I am remembering when we were young. We would walk up the hill and into the thick patch of sumacs. There we would lay on our backs in the warm sunshine and let the clouds hypnotize us with flowers and swans and angels. Within the wonderful bounds of imagination, I was a happy child.

We would walk around the bend past the station and wait for the train. I loved the trains so much, to me they represented all that was big and powerful. You and I would go walking down the tracks for miles and miles, singing songs and making up stories.. We made a contest out of looking for shiny and pretty stones and we would pick them up and let Granny decide who won. It was usually me, but after all, Granny was biased. On a really good day, we would find a patch of violets in the woods, or a four leafed clover, or some mushrooms.

We would make up poems but would giggle too much to recite them; and remember when we would tie the boys shoe laces together in the back shed and then run like hell laughing our heads off? Yes, there were some happy times and I think that in my misery, I hid them away in the back of my mind so that the only thoughts of my past were sad or bitter or hating. I am not blaming myself, I was only a child and as a child, had no control of what was going on in my life. I only had my imagination to turn to for happiness and even then, I really didn't know what the word happiness meant, but we did have happy days, didn't we?

Now, I can feel free of my childhood, free of my

117

blunders in marriage, free of all the ghosts and monsters that have haunted me. Has it been worth the journey, Oh God, yes. I have so much to be happy and thankful for. I have my sons, my grandchildren, a job to go to, an apartment to come home to, my paintings, poems and plants, and all the pretty little rocks that we have gathered over the years. Now, when I get down, I think of the beautiful faces of my grandchildren and I smile.

Love Maggie.

January 1, 2003

Dear Jennifer, Following is a piece that I have kept for many years and I still love it. Because I love it, here it is.

~Recipe for a Happy New Year~

Take twelve fine, full-grown months. Select only those which are thoroughly free from all old memories of bitterness, rancor, hate and jealousy. Clean them completely free from every clinging spite. Pick off all specs of pettiness and narrowness of mind. In short, see that each of these months is freed from all the past so that they are as fresh and clean as when they first came from the great storehouse of time.

Next, cut these months into thirty or thirty-one equal parts. They will keep for only one year, so do not attempt to make up the whole batch at one time. Rather, prepare one day at a time.

Into each day, put twelve parts of faith, eleven

of patience, ten of courage, nine of work (some people omit this ingredient and so spoil the flavor of the rest,) eight of hope, seven of fidelity, six of liberality, five of kindness, four of rest (leaving this one out is like leaving the dressing out of the salad), three of prayer, two of meditation, and one part only of selected resolution. For spice and sweetening, according to our scruples, add about a teaspoonful of good spirits, a dash of fun, a pinch of folly, a sprinkle of play and a heaping cup of good humor. Pour love, liberally, into the whole and mix. Cook thoroughly then garnish with a few smiles and a sprig of joy. Then be sure to serve with unselfishness and cheerfulness and a happy year is a certainty.

Remember, with a smile and a prayer, twelve new and wonderfully glorious months have been issued in your name to do with as you wish. Father Time has signed your note and it is negotiable on January 1st.

If you make a mistake, be sure you don't make the same one over again. Laugh at difficulties, and they will soon vanish. Attempt to carry heavier responsibilities and you will find them growing lighter. Face a bad situation and it will clear up. Tell the truth and find an easier way out. Do an honest-to-God day's work every day and reap the rewards. Believe that people are honest, and you will find them living up to your expectations. Trust in God each day that every step you take will be guided by his goodness, mercy, and love.

Love, Maggie

CHAPTER TWENTY ONE

DO UNTO OTHERS

" Doing nothing for others is the undoing of one's self. We must be purposely kind and generous or we miss the best part of life's existence. The heart that goes out of itself gets large and full of joy and love. This is the great secret of the inner life. We do ourselves most good by doing something for others."

Horace Mann

8. By your own attitude and the way you treat others, show others how to treat you. Show them how you want to be treated. Karma, - what goes around comes around, "Do unto others as you would have them do unto you. . ." - love with all your heart and love will be returned to you - believe in it, it is true. Most important, when you see others playing the same parts as you once played, have and show some understanding, empathy and compassion. So far in your life, you have tried to receive the love and attention that you craved and never received as a child, now you are at peace with the universe, reach out to others and give thanks each and every day of your life.

March 20, 2003

Dear Jenny,

It has been a while, I know, but I had to think pretty hard to figure out how my attitude has effected the way people treat me. I have always treated people with compassion and respect, but I am afraid that people haven't treated me that way. The reality is that I can only be as understanding and compassionate to others to the degree that I am understanding and compassionate to myself. So actually, I have been treating people with a false compassion always firstly seeking approval and "brownie points" for myself.

If I meet a person that I don't like, that is my problem. No-one in the whole world is going to change her personality just so that I will like her. By the same token if a person doesn't like me that is her problem. Taking for granted that everyone in the world is living her life to the best of her knowledge and experience, who am I to judge if others are right or wrong.

As children, we were taught to take everything that happened in our lives and everything that was said to us not only seriously, but to the extreme. We were continually poised to defend ourselves or run. As we were only small children, we had no choices for defending ourselves. If we even tried to defend ourselves verbally, our situation became worse, so we learned to keep quiet, but stay on guard.

Through living our lives in constant crisis, we took on the idea that the whole world was in constant crisis, and that we must stay defensive and bitter. As we became adults, our lives stayed defensive and bitter, our emotions constantly venerable and ready to be hurt, or put down, or laughed at, or bullied. Even when given a compliment, we would look for an ulterior motive. This makes for a very sad and cranky person.

If we walk around sad and cranky, guess what, people will treat us sad and cranky. If we are cheerful, smiling and happy, people will treat us that way, but we must realize that we would always rather do what we want to do, not what we have to do. In other words, if we want to be treated well, we have to want to live well.

Because my father was a cruel authoritarian, another problem I have always had to battle was being afraid of the boss or anyone in authority. If I am called into the boss's office, I am nervous and extremely uncomfortable. I automatically presume I have done something wrong and again, as when I was a child, I prepare myself for violence. How I can overcome this is to repeat to myself over and over again, "I am a calm and confident worker, I do a good job. I deserve to be praised for my work. My boss is a good person, I like her." Over again, I will affirm my place at work.

I live alone because I want to live alone. I am happy to live alone. I would much rather live alone and give myself respect, peace, serenity and dignity than to live with a partner in a sick relationship. To be honest, I am not ready yet to even think of another man in my life. So many women can't live without a man. If that is the case, they (for sure) need to work on living alone. For so many years, I was so full of hate for the fact that my father had crippled me, that I thought he didn't deserve my forgiveness. He damaged me right to the core of my soul and without any concern or remorseful feelings, he died. He couldn't have cared less that I needed so much to forgive him. However, if I were to overcome any of the atrocities of my past, I had to forgive him. It is not about my Dad, it is about me! I also refused to let him win. I refused to be the person that he had molded me into, I refused to be bitter and afraid and tied to my past and therefore bound to him. By forgiving him, I set myself free.

I finally realized that I am the one who chooses how I feel. My behavior depends on my perception and my interpretation of the world around me. So, if I choose to stay bitter and live with my heart and soul full of hate, that is entirely up to me. If I choose to drink my life away and live in the gutter, that is also up to me. At any moment in time, we are exactly where we want to be. If not, we would do something to change our lives. Many say "no, I can't change my life, I am a victim of life, a victim of abuse, I don't want to change because if I don't, I can wallow in self pity, expect people to feel sorry for me and take care of me." Maybe like me, she will gain her understanding and her change will come late in life. Hopefully not, hopefully with all the information available she will find a way and have the courage find peace.

People quite often use the atrocities of their childhood as an excuse to drink or medicate in any way so they don't have to feel the pain. They often say, " oh yes, that's what's her name. She was raped you know as a youngster, so don't blame her for the drunkenness or any other way she is letting herself down." Or, "yes, they took her children away. Not her fault, you know she was being abused." Again, we have to take responsibility for our own lives. There is no excuse for our thoughts and actions. If we continue to use our misfortunes as reasons for addictions, we will continue to suffer. But it is our own choice. If we are to find happiness, we have to stop blaming, accept and understand our lives.

It is very kind, but not wise to think that we have the power and the love to change our abusers. The fact is that it won't happen. If he wanted to change, he would get help himself. If you choose to stay with your abuser then you are contributing to your own misery. You don't need to be kind to him, you need to be kind to yourself. It's his problem, but if you decide to stay, it is your problem too.

Lost

We have walked and walked
sometimes hand in hand, sometimes miles apart.
Struggling endlessly thru thick undergrowth
or happily roaming thru the green pastures.
But darkness fell and we couldn't see,
we didn't know where to go.
Darkness can confuse us for
we seel things in the dark that are not real,
that we can't understand.
Should we stumble along in the dark,
hoping for a light to guide us?
Or should we walk our separate paths
and find the dawn?

~CHAPTER TWENTY TWO~

BULLIES

"Anybody can become angry. That is not difficult, but to be angry with the right person to the right degree, and at the right time, and for the right purpose, and in the right way: that is not within everyone's grasp and is not easy. To keep anger inside and to redirect it on innocent people is to become a bully, an abuser."
Aristotle

April 5, 2003

Dear Jenny,

I have been reading more and more as time goes by, and as time goes by I understand more and more.

How does all this start? Where does it start and when? Do children have "addictive or abusive personalities"? Can a child of ten or twelve have already formed a violent, angry temperament? Is he acting out his feelings and pushing kids around because he feels powerless in his own life? Firstly, if this child was raised with abuse , violence, and anger, then there is a good chance that the child will become either an abuser or a victim.

It starts in the womb and it continues to grow and flourish along with the child. Take a look at a ten year old school yard bully. Isn't what he or she is doing a junior version of the abusive parent? By using power in the form of verbal abuse, and physical force, he fulfils his need for power by forcing other children into submission.   He takes lunch money, toys, hockey cards and whatever else he can get away with and simply finds joy and power in pushing and shoving other kids around. Being powerful gives him a huge "rush", he feels fantastic.   He gains power over all of his pent up aggression and hate toward those who have abused him, or abandoned him, or taken away his self esteem. This "rush" is similar to the one felt when one is watching an old cowboy movie and one cowboy punches the other. That whack is the rush.   People who love this type of rush are ones who attend boxing matches and love to see a fight in a hockey game. The bully picks on children smaller than he just as the person abusing him is bigger than he. After he has felt the "rush", and gotten away with it, he does it again and then again as the aggressive tension builds up within him, and soon he is a full fledged abuser.

While still in the womb, the child can hear and feel the emotions of the mother feeling stressed. Just as he can hear soft soothing music, he can also hear loud frightening noises of people shouting. He also feels the shock of a physical blow to the mother and the fear and tension and stress of the mother.

He is born into the horrible world of family violence.   The violence he lives with leaves him constantly fearful and powerless, the more he is bullied, the more hate and aggression he stores within. He takes out his lack of power on others. He quiet often drops out of high school as his relationship with teachers is poor, they represent power therefore he lacks respect for them. His relationship with other students is still one of bullying, and cursing and yelling, so both teachers and other students are not unhappy to see him drop out. Quite often he starts drinking or doping. He doesn't have a job and his parent(s) boot him out. He starts stealing to support his addiction(s) and quite often ends up in the gutter or in jail. As with most people, sooner or later, he meets and lives with a partner and has a family. Now he has his own victim and children to bully and beat on - and on and on it goes.

Bullying, like abuse and family violence are problems that are not even near to being solved. In fact bullying problems are very common in the schools all across the nation, and instead of getting better, they are getting worse. In many towns and cities, parents have formed committees to come up with ideas and ways to stop the bullying. I think we will see no great change until abuse of any kind is no longer acceptable behavior in our society. That takes education and non-acceptance. It takes total equality for women and stronger punishments for those who choose to hurt and hit and kill them.

It is really amazing, Jen the more I understand, the more my whole life comes together like a jigsaw puzzle where before, the pieces wouldn't fit, so the picture was distorted. But now, it all goes together so easily and I see everything so clearly.

Gotta go,
love Maggie

Silence

Silence is golden, sometimes.
Sometimes it means there is nothing left to say;
or I hate you, and don't want to talk; or
I love you and words are not necessary.
I am ignoring you and I want you to go away,
or I need you, don't leave me.
I have dark, horrible secrets
and if I tell you, you will hate me
or you will be disgusted and leave me.
When there are no words,
silence can mean I know how you feel, or
I have no idea, or I just don't care.
The silence goes on, the secrets are kept.
Be aware of silence, sometimes it is not golden.

April 10, 2003

Dear Jenny,

In this world where love, peace and tolerance are part of our society, how do we continue to accept family violence and abuse as part of life? How do we pretend it doesn't happen?

It used to be that all families had their skeletons in the closet. Anything from pregnancy, abortions, being gay, retarded, mentally ill, wife bashing, drug and/or alcohol problems were hidden from public view. Secrets were never told if they brought any speck of shame to the family. All families were expected to be upstanding and proud. It was pride that would cause the little children who were being beaten and raped and verbally abused and mentally and emotionally scarred to never, ever tell, and therefore keeping all that stuff hidden inside where it would continue to boil up and fester until the person either becomes totally submissive, or extremely and/or totally aggressive. The submissive ones become the victims, and the aggressive ones become the abusers, many of them become monsters.

If a person has been abused, it is a law of the universe that in order to heal, she has to tell. She cannot keep secrets and find peace in life. If she doesn't tell, the universe will punish her with all the pain and agony that goes along with keeping the secret. The whole thing will eat at her as she goes on from day to day, year to year living with the secrets and knowing that her purpose in life, her happiness, her peace of mind will never happen. She must talk to someone, call someone, get some help, but no-one can do it for her, she must do it herself. Sometimes it is easier to talk to a complete stranger. If there is a toll free line in the phone book, an abuse help line, she must call and at try, at least attempt to talk.

We are all human beings. Not one of us is totally pure and untouched by this world. There should be not one thing in our lives that we are unable to talk about. If there is, we are keeping secrets and secrets hurt, they fester. Many times a woman will say they lost a child in infancy, or lost a sibling, or had an abortion, or been raped, but they don't talk about it because it hurts. That hurt will eventually cause much greater pain, but they could talk about it and accept it and go on.
Sorry for rambling, Love Maggie

April 25, 2003

Dear Jennifer,

It is true, the more I learn, the more I understand what has happened in my life and in the lives of others. In the case of victims of abuse, it is hard to imagine the suffering that takes place physically as well as mentally and spiritually. Many people believe that our body, mind and soul are all connected by our spirit. Therefore if the body is suffering so is the mind and soul and all three need to be healed, not just the body.

When a person lives in constant and extreme stress, her body functions differently than those of other people. Her heart beats faster, her blood pressure is higher, the adrenaline is pumping constantly in preparation for crisis - all the time. This makes her body work overtime - all the time. She is in such crisis, that she can't think properly, well aware that the next words she speaks may bring on violence. She sleeps, not relaxed, but with her mind and body poised for violence. She wakes often during the night and wakes still stressed and tired with her muscles in knots .

Imagine what this is doing to her heart. Stress is a major cause of heat attack and stroke. She likely medicates herself with alcohol and cigarettes which she thinks are giving her relief from stress but actually add to the physical dangers of her condition.

Her stomach reacts to stress by producing too much acid which causes ulcers. Her bowels quite often also develop ulcers and therefor colitis or irritable bowel syndrome caused by mucus and toxins in the intestines.

She may eat too much or too little, her weight may be way under, or way over the optimum for her age and height.

She may suffer from a number of neurological or psychological disorders like panic, migraine, eating disorders, re-occurring depression, fears and phobias of many kinds and to many degrees of intensity.

This is one sick girl.   Her abuser is even more sick. Leaving her abuser is the hardest decision she will have to make in her life.   It means that she will be forcing herself to be a person, not a door mat. It will cause huge and often overwhelming stress. As she begins to heal, she begins to gain tiny bits of courage and as time goes by, the pain isn't as hard to bare and she begins to feel better.   Hopefully she finds a safe place to go for herself and her children. She sleeps in peace, knowing she is safe.   She can begin to make plans for her future that include being happy. She can see a doctor or councillor without having to feel guilty or be put down. She can get real medication (not booze) for depression and she can detoxify without interference from her partner.

Hopefully her abuser will hit bottom and start a journey of his own. But that is all up to him. She can't allow herself and shouldn't feel in any way responsible for what her abuser does now or has ever done. If she is to emerge as a Survivor, she has to break the ties and move forward in her life.   If she really wants to help him, and all people are worth helping, she should give him the space to help himself.

 'Nuff for now!

Love Maggie

Was that my life -

That just passed me by on the inside lane?
Was that it?
Nearly sixty years in such a short, short time?
Was that what I worried and fussed about,
cried and lied about?
Wanted out of, or more of
or less of or something greater than,
was that really my purpose?
Was that my life, the years
I saw thru rose colored glasses
or the bottom of a wine glass?
Did it take so many years to
drink up that bottle and
survive that hangover?
When did my children grow up, and
become real, big people?
When did they grow taller than me
and warmer than me and wiser than me?
When did they tear down the outhouse
and stop using horses on the farm?
I don't understand -
I must have missed it,
my life just passed me by
in such a short, short time
and I never learned to dance.

May 2, 2003

Dear Jenny,

It will soon be my birthday and it's funny, but I don't mind getting old anymore. When I look in the mirror now, I see my wrinkles and double chin and I smile at myself, because they are signs of maturity. I feel much more beautiful now than I did twenty years ago. My smile is real, genuine, it shows my happiness.

Even now, at times, I feel that I can't let anyone get close to me. I feel fear and guilt if someone shows me love or empathy or compassion. Maybe I still feel that I am undeserving? I don't know. I know that I don't want to bring all of this baggage into someone else's life. I don't want to ask for forgiveness ever again. The pain is unbearable, it hurts too much.

I do know that healing takes a long time, and I will continue to work toward healing and eventually I will be whole. I have found great peace in my life, a feeling of contentment and serenity. I feel that it is good for people to live alone if they are hurting. Living alone has allowed me to face up to myself, to cry it out, to live without the pressure to be someone other than myself and to bit by bit sort out my life. It is a necessity to learn to live with yourself, to learn to love yourself and to have the peace and quiet in your life allow yourself to do that.

I used to keep away from men because I was so afraid. Afraid of emotional intimacy, afraid that my old feelings of I have to do as I am told. Afraid that if a man said "take your clothes off and lie down" that I would, whether I wanted to or not, because I was still afraid of being hurt. That fear was huge.

If I do ever have another relationship, I want it to go slow. I don't want to feel pressured into sex or to feel that money is in any way part of love. I don't want to look for a relationship, I want it to find me. I want to feel that I deserve to be loved and happy and then little by little find true intimacy.

Love, Maggie

P. S. There's no fool like an old fool! I feel now that I have gained the knowledge and maturity that if I did find love, I would know from my heart if it was right for me or not. It is true, men know if a women is looking for a man. Apparently we have a look, and aura, it is supposed to have something to do with hormones and when you get to my age, and your hormone days are done, it has something to do with compatibility and companionship. - Maggie

May 22, 2003

Dear Jennifer,

I feel now that I am ready to start the ninth step. It may sound simple, but it isn't, because it causes me to again bring up the past. I don't want to live in the past, I want to live today and look forward to tomorrow. I want to show people that I am a deserving person, that I am no longer the sad, depressed unloving victim that I used to be. That is why it is hard to look back. - I will try, you know I will. M.

~CHAPTER TWENTY THREE~

HEALING

"Who will tell whether one happy moment of love, or the joy of breathing or walking on a bright warm morning and the smelling of fresh air, is not worth all the effort which life implies. It is not then the suffering that counts in life, but the healing." Erich Fromm

9. As you feel yourself healing, you will know, it will occur to you that you are becoming more and more a survivor and less and less a victim. Keep a notebook and in it write down every time it occurs to you that what you are doing, thinking, feeling, what you fantasize, your attitudes toward others and toward yourself that are a result of your childhood. In this way, you can clarify how far you have come and how far you still have to go. Happiness and peace of mind are a lifetime effort. Some start off on the right road as a child, some don't get to the road until they are into the golden years. It really doesn't matter. You realize now that the past is far behind you and that tomorrow holds great promise. If you live for today, to be happy today, you have found the road to reality and that road will lead you home.

"Today is that tomorrow you thought of yesterday."

Reality

There is no reality, only perception;
truth is as we interpret it.
A picture is only as I see it.
My life is only as I live it.
If I see and perceive my life
thru my own eyes
it must be my own reality,
therefore,
would you like to hear the truth
or some beautiful lies?

June 1, 2003

Dear Jenny,

Saying "I'm sorry" became an acceptable habit with me. I was sorry for every little thing, if I cough, or sneeze, if I think I have interrupted, if I think I have said the wrong thing, I am sorry. Feeling sorry results in feeling guilty, guilt is hard to live with. As a child, I was always told that everything I did or said, I must be sorry for, just in case. There was no pleasing my father, no making him happy. As a result, I feel guilty if I sleep or "waste time" relaxing. I was always taught that sleeping in, or taking a nap was wasting time, that I could have better used that time doing something more productive. Sometimes I feel that same guilt when I am painting, art is not work, and should not be done if there are chores to do. Actually, everything I would do for myself I felt guilty about. Every time I would spend money or go out, or treat myself in any way the guilt far outweighed the pleasure, so I would avoid doing anything for myself.

Now, I do and go where I want to. I have learned to be kind to myself and all the guilt that I have felt over the years has only hurt me, therefore, it belongs in the garbage. I realize now that when I am tempted to jump into a conversation and add some tid bit to make me look good, I let it go and consciously keep my mouth shut, for which I feel people have much more respect and I respect myself for doing it.

Lying was a big part of our childhood. We lied about all sorts of things, especially at school. We would have people believing that we had all sorts of wonderful things, lovely clothes, fine furniture, a close loving family, anything to keep them from the truth. We also lied constantly to the Monster to keep ourselves safe and out of trouble. We did it for the most part in order to survive our childhood. Living in our imagination also became part of the survival, which added to our lying. Breaking old habits is very hard. As we grew to be adults, we quite often found that our imaginations were still working overtime. Regurgitation the past was very painful after all, secrets had to be kept, dirty laundry was not to be hung out. The imagination could offer us several other options and many of the lies told while we were young, stayed with us throughout our lives. For instance, when I left my father's house, I had turned sixteen two weeks before. To get a job of any kind, I had to be a high school graduate that would put me at eighteen. I lied on both counts and got a job. I have no need to lie any more, the truth is wonderful.

I have been through so much poverty so many

times, it is my nature not to waste, especially food or money. I remember well not having either. So many years ago, Jenny, you and I would play parts in Gone With The Wind. I will never forget how I practiced over and over the one line when Scarlet goes back to Tara "I will never go hungry again". I did go hungry again, but for the sake of survival. I know even if I were a millionaire, I would have some little stash of cash hidden somewhere so that I would not have to go hungry again.

I still have a huge need to be loved, to be recognized and appreciated. I grew up as somewhat less than a human being, not loved and not accepted as a person. That is why I grew up in my imagination, but if it were not for my imagination, I would not have grown into the very creative person that I am. I would not be able to see the colors and scenes with my artist eyes, hear the poetry that is all around me, or have the creative drive to be a writer. In fact I may not have survived.

On Father's day I still have such sad feelings. Oh how I wish I'd had a Daddy. The feeling passes quickly now, and every year I count my blessings and feel such happiness in knowing that my son is such a wonderful Daddy. He loves his children so much, the joy is indescribable. If I shed a tear on Father's day, it is because I feel so proud and I thank God that the horrible disease called abuse will not be passed down through the generations of my family. Knowing this is what makes my life worthwhile. I have learned that fear can eat away at your very soul. I have learned that not all dogs bite; not all open spaces are threatening; not all closets have spiders; not all men lash out and not all guns kill. I have learned that I need to face life unafraid and as I accomplish that, then I can face death unafraid.

What brings me joy and makes my life wonderful, what do I love who do I love? I love my children and grandchildren, my brothers, sisters, their families and my Mom. I love the sounds of my grand-children laughing and playing, growing up carefree and unafraid. I love sheets that have been dried on a clothesline, oatmeal with brown sugar, mashed turnips, poached eggs and good friends. I love plants and flowers and Opra. I love trees, looking up into the branches and feeling their power. I love the smell of fresh cut grass, burning leaves and the sunshine late on a winter afternoon. I love the old 50's and 60's music, Roy Orbison and Patsy Cline.

I look forward to the future, to whatever time the good Lord gives me. I want to make the best of that time, make my days happy and my nights serene and restful and now I know that only I can accomplish this. When I die, I want to die peacefully and simply pass from this world, hopefully with a smile.

Over the years, our expectations of life change, and time gives a wonderful gift of healing. It gives back to us in later years what we have missed in childhood.

No, Jenny, I will not be writing again. I know we made a vow when we were nine that we would never grow up, but I am all grown up now. After all is said and done, one thing I do know, if I could have done any better in my life, I would have, I did as all people do, the best I could. Good bye, Jennifer, my best friend.
Love, Maggie

EPILOGUE:

Granny was right, there did come a day when I no longer needed Jennifer and she did let me go to live a life of my own. Granny and Jennifer lived only in my imagination and looking back now, maybe I wouldn't have become a survivor without them. Granny provided a mentor who was kind and wise and cared about me. When I needed to ask an adult what was right or how to act, I would ask Granny. She never hit me, never shouted and she loved me unconditionally. Why Granny? Because I really did have one, two actually, but they both may as well have lived a thousand miles away.

Although Jennifer lived only in my imagination, she was really my best friend. How sane is that? The truth is, she kept me sane. No matter what, she was always there when I had no one else to be my friend, I could tell her anything and she understood. As with all best friends, we would have spats and make up and do all the things that little girls do. As an adult, she became the person that I told all my dirty little secrets to and she helped me so much just by being there. For the longest time, five years in fact, she was the only person in the world (real or imagined) who could totally accept and understand me and if I were to become a survivor, I really needed understanding, I needed a guardian angel and her name was Jennifer.

Guardian Angel

*My angel watches over me
in times of sadness and despair.
She is strong and courageous
And when I am full of pain,
she is gentle and kind,
and knowing and wise,
and calm and peaceful
when the world is full
of chaos and hate.
My angel is close and loving,
a sister sharing every day
giving to me a legacy of love
and understanding,
of forgiveness and joy,
living on inside my heart,
my angel is me.*

THE END